RECIPE OF GOD

Omri Meir Serper

Copyright © 2018 by Omri Meir Serper

ISBN 9781717902108

ALL RIGHTS RESERVED

No part of this publication may be reproduced, stored in a retrieval system, or transmitted in any for or by any means, electronic, mechanical, photocopying, recording, or otherwise, without prior written permission. Scanning, uploading, and distributing this book via the internet or by other means without the permission of the author and publisher is illegal. Please respect the authors rights and do not participate in or encourage piracy of copyrighted material.

Preface

This book was written with the intention of engaging both the religious and secular mind.
After reading and understanding this book, you will be able to draw your own conclusions, based on facts presented. You will have all the information you need to make moral decisions easily, have the curtain lifted on some of the misleading ways you were taught, and revisit things you experienced in your life with a new clarity.

The wish to understand the real recipe for a good life, given to us from God, had sent me on a quest. Getting into the depth of things to uncover facts was always a part of my nature and in this book I am bringing out the full story with a different angle. In this book, I share with you the facts I discovered that led me to my current lifestyle and changed my life for the better and will, I hope, help you to make the same changes.

Through the trails of life, I have been to many different places, experienced different people, different traditions, different cultures and different tastes. Most individuals, as they navigate through life, come to the understanding that people (now and in the past), despite their many differences, are ultimately the same in their core. It is the choices each of us makes individually and as part of a group that divide or unite us and create positive changes or negative changes in the world. It is all a matter of choice.

It is up to Mankind to choose the way forward and make decision that will affect the condition of the world. The future of The Earth, the future of The Seas, the future of The Sky and All living creatures depend on the choices we make today.

By uncovering hidden wisdom this book will give you inspiration to improve your life and tools to influence others.

Chapter 1

Back to the routes

Since Mankind first walked The Earth, according to the first monotheistic religion, God gave them the Mental and Physical nutrition that would keep them pure. A recipe which contained no evil nor destruction in it. Healthy and full of every ingredient mankind needed in order to live at a pure divinity level as mentioned in Genesis 1, 26.

Due to one wrong turn on Mankind's path of thinking, many false trails were created and followed leading to the misguided route the world has taken and is on today.

To understand how to get back to the original, authentic and pure recipe given to us by God, there is a crucial need to decode the ancient writings and understand the true meaning of the letters, words, sentences and numbers leading to true mastery of the full story. The true meaning of the original ancient Hebrew text was revealed by the ancient sages but lost through a trail of Mistranslations from the original Hebrew of the Torah and the Koine Greek of the New Testament to the various modern languages they are read in today.

Chapter 2

Since the beginning of time

God created all the living creatures of The Earth and "saw" that they were good. It was the beginning of Intelligent life. Before mankind was created, there was an open range, a gate-less, fence-less heaven for the blessed creations of God.

God's creations all have a part in perfecting the world that is still developing step by step, organism by organism. These creations were blessed by God and are not ours to disturb, nor destroy.

To please itself, mankind created a wall of lies and deceptions which has taken a huge toll on Heaven and Earth. This wall of lies and deceptions hides the true path and prevents us from reaching the divinity level that is our birthright.

Most people intuitively know and see the wrongs but keep ignoring them, claiming, incorrectly, that they are a necessary part of modern life or justifying them as cultural/religious traditions.

It is time to let our brothers and sisters know that we were led down the wrong path and it is time for us, all together, to change our ways. All of us together can change the world for the better.

This change will bring us closer to the divinity level, the world mankind was originally born into.

Let us have the moral strength and will to come back to our first and authentic being as the creation of God, made in his image and with his character.

Let mankind know that words are not enough, actions are needed to uncover what our mind and soul desire. Do not be the one who prays for others, when they do not pray for themselves. Deeds must be done.

Ezekiel 33:31

לא ויבואו אליך כמבוא־עם וישבו לפניך עמי ושמעו את־דבריך ואותם לא יעשו כי־עגבים בפיהם המה עשים אחרי בצעם לבם הלך

And come unto thee as the people come, and sit before thee as

My people, and hear thy words, but do them not - for with their

mouth they show much love, but their heart goes after their greed.

Chapter 3

Original state of mind.

To understand where mankind got lost and how we can find ourselves, we must observe and understand the beginning. Below is the seven day creation story translated exactly as it appears in the original Hebrew, with no modern interpretations or mistranslations.

The creation was God's original plan for his creations and the way we were meant to live. It is also the closest we were ever to God. In this story, God lays out his recipe for living truly in his image, a life that is in harmony with everything else he created and that is a part of him.

I encourage you to read this as if for the first time. Notice that "living soul" and "live soul" is not an expression used only for humans. It is used to describe "every Earth animal".

The creation.

Day 1
Earth was chaos, there was nothingness and darkness.
The spirit of god was floating above the waters
Between The Waters of top and bottom.
And God said, let there be light and there was light: God saw the light as good and distinguished the light from darkness: and God has called the light – Morning and to the darkness – Night.

Day 2
A skyline was created to differentiate between the upper waters and the lower waters.
The waters above were separated and called sky.

Day 3
The waters under the skyline will go into one place and the land will be seen. The waters will be called seas and the land will be called earth.
God said let the earth sprout vegetation, seed bearing herb, [and] fruit trees of every kind that have seeds in them and [so] on the earth the land pulled out vegetation, seed bearing herb in all kinds, and fruit trees which have their own seeds in all kinds.

Day 4
Creation of the different lights in the skyline to separate between morning and night and they will use for signs, dates, days and years. The big light was created for the morning and the smaller light and stars for the night. God had given them in the skyline to light upon earth,
To govern in morning and night and to distinguish between light and darkness.

Day 5
And God said, let the water swarm with **living soul** swarms and birds will fly on the earth in the skyline of the sky. And God has created the big alligators (Dinosaurs) and all the soul creatures that swarm in the water in all kinds and all the winged birds in all their kinds.
God has blessed the sea creatures and birds with fertility and increasing in numbers, fill the waters in the seas and fill the earth.

Day 6

God has said the earth will bring out **living souls in their kinds,** Cattle, Creeping livings and Wild animal in every kind. And God has created the wild animals in all kinds, the cattle in its kinds and all the short legged and crawlers of the ground in its kinds.

Then God said: We will make a human in our image, in our figure and they will rule all fish of the sea, birds of the sky, cattle and all the land and all the short-legged insects and crawlers on the ground.

God did make a human in his own image, man and woman he has created them, blessed them and told them: be fertile and increase your numbers and conquer the earth and rule the fish of the sea, birds of the sky and every animal that walks the earth.

And God Says:

Here, I give you all seed-bearing herb that is upon all the earth and every seed-bearing fruit tree, will be for you to eat.
And for every earth animal and for every bird of the sky and every creature that is upon the earth, which have a live soul in them, all vegetable herbs will be for food.
And God saw all that he has done and it was Very good.

Day 7

Everything God made, was completed and God rested from all his work and made the seventh day holy, for it was the day he had rested from the creation labor.

Chapter 4

Easy Answer and Hard Question

God blessed his creations and his creations were blessed. The Words which were given to us by God, should be respected and kept with total devotion. The full story we are told is how we should live.

God Says:
Here, I give you all seed-bearing herb that is upon all the earth and every seed-bearing fruit tree, will be for you to eat.
And for every earth animal and for every bird of the sky and every creature that is upon the earth, which has a live soul in them, all vegetable herbs will be for food (Day 6 in God's creation).

We can clearly see from this passage that it was God's intention for mankind to only feed on earth's fruit, vegetables and herbs. Then why are we eating meat? Is it the way we should live our life? Is it the way people who want to be closer to God should live? Do we have the will to adopt a better and more Moral approach to feeding ourselves? What needs to happen to change the current hunter mindset, which drives the negative behavioral patterns most of us follow in the modern world? How can we end the exploitation of God's creations, elevate our spirituality, and become closer to The Divinity Level?

Most people would say they are animal lovers and would never directly harm one, however, every day most people make choices that contribute to their unimaginable suffering. In many cases people are unaware of the harm they cause through deliberate manipulation by big corporations in the name of greed, through familial and societal pressure, and through cultural traditions. Even animals on Humane Farms are suffering and nothing humane happens in a slaughterhouse. Whether it is for fashion, entertainment, food, or religion our treatment of animals has become abusive and we are not protecting and caring for God's creatures as were directed to.

Unconsciously it has become the norm to support abuse directly and indirectly. How can we return to the pure divinity level and live a healthy and valuable life? How do we stop the abuse of God's creations, who are bred and raised for the sole purpose of dying? Once we become aware that animals we have designated as "food" were never meant for us to consume, because they do not belong to us and are simply under our care as God's representatives on Earth, we will stop treating the way we do today
.

It would be considered inhumane and depraved to impregnate a woman only to take her baby away after birth so that her breast milk could be bottled and sold yet we consider it normal if the mother and child are not human. What about the daily murdering of animals in the name of sport, fun and bonding? Clearly it is time for us as a society to take action.

Ask yourself, do I wish to go back to moral purity? How will I contribute to the fight for God's creations' rights and life? Whether religious or secular, our moral obligation is to protect and care for creatures we share this planet with, from the smallest creature upon the earth to mankind itself, we must wake up and change our ways. We must strive to get back to our origin; living in harmony with animals.

When we take matters of life and death into our own hands and decide to disturb and destroy instead of nurture and heal, there is an urgent need for a change.

Chapter 5

The importance of meaning

When we read The Bible, it is critical to keep in mind that it is a translation from the original Hebrew, which did not include any punctuation (like periods, commas, paragraphs, verses, etc) or Nikud Taberni (vowels). The lack of punctuation and vowels allowed for mistakes, manipulations, and wildly different translations that have led to many misinterpretations. In the following chapters I will reveal how several critical portions of The Bible have been mistranslated and how that has resulted in completely incorrect interpretations, which, in turn, have led to misunderstandings and the incorrect teaching of its contents.

When we read The Bible in a language besides Hebrew, we are often presented with words that are translated in a way that brings a different meaning to the whole sentence than was intended and shows us the light in a different tone and paints us a picture with a different tincture. Bible readers do not always understand what they read, due to mistranslations, misguidance and wrong teachings. Most religious figures and instructors have never read the original text in the original Hebrew and are therefore inadvertently filling the students' minds with wrong ideas and twisting the story. These same teachers are simply passing forward the misguided and incorrect information they were taught and took at face value. Remember the word of the wise,

"For verily I say unto you, till heaven and earth pass away, one jot (*jot - also written as yod - is the smallest Hebrew letter in the alphabet*) or one tittle shall in no wise pass from the law, till all be fulfilled". (Matthew 5;18)

As you can see, Jesus himself declared that the word of God will never change; not even one 'Yod' (the smallest Hebrew letter) or 'Tittle' (the smallest detail) from God's law, until all things are accomplished and fulfilled.

As in previous chapters, you will see the critical words and sentences, whose incorrect translation changed the original meaning and teachings, **bolded** to emphasize the difference. To completely understand the story, one can not separate quotes, nor pick one from here and one from there to create one's own version. Follow the bold words and sentences, one after the other and the true meaning of the story shall be uncovered and the original version revealed.

Chapter 6

Understanding Noah's wrong

Most everyone grows up learning the story of Noah and the flood. What some, but not everyone, also learns is that this story includes God giving humans permission to murder and eat animals. This is actually false and a result of a mistranslation by those who were from a culture of eating flesh.

The passages below include bolded and underlined portions that are meant to help you understand the story as it is actually written but often not how it is told. I encourage you to read this slowly and carefully as if for the very first time.

After giving you the story in its entirety, I will then go through the most important passages and explain their meaning by digging into the original text and its translations (and mistranslations).

6.9	**This is the history of Noah.** Noah was a man righteous and innocent in his generations; Noah walked with God.	אלה תולדת נח נח איש צדיק תמים היה בדרתיו את האלהים התהלך נח
6.11	And **the earth was corrupt before God, and the earth was filled with violence.**	ותשחת הארץ לפני האלהים ותמלא הארץ חמס
6.12	And God saw the earth, and,	וירא אלהים את הארץ והנה

	behold, it was corrupt; for **all flesh had corrupted their way** upon the earth.	נשחתה כי השחית כל בשר את דרכו על הארץ
6.13	And God said unto Noah: 'The end of **all flesh** is come before Me; for the earth is filled with violence through them; and I will destroy them with the earth.	ויאמר אלהים לנח קץ כל בשר בא לפני כי מלאה הארץ חמס מפניהם והנני משחיתם את הארץ
6.19	And of **every animal of all flesh**, two of every sort shalt thou bring into the ark, **to keep them alive with thee**; they shall be male and female.	ומכל החי מכל בשר שנים מכל תביא אל התבה להחית אתך זכר ונקבה יהיו
6.20	Of the **birds to their kind**, and of **the cattle to their kind**, of **every creep of the ground to its kind**, two of every sort shall come unto thee, to **keep them alive.**	מהעוף למינהו ומן הבהמה למינה מכל רמש האדמה למינהו שנים מכל יבאו אליך להחיות
6.21	And **take** thou unto thee of **all food that is eaten**, and gather it to thee; and **it shall be for food for thee, and for them.**'	ואתה קח לך מכל מאכל אשר יאכל ואספת אליך והיה לך ולהם לאכלה
6.22	**Thus did Noah; as to all that God commanded him, so did he.**	ויעש נח ככל אשר צוה אתו אלהים כן עשה

7.1	And the Lord said unto Noah: 'Come thou and all thy house into the ark; for thee have I seen righteous before Me in this generation.	ויאמר יהוה לנח בא אתה וכל ביתך אל התבה כי אתך ראיתי צדיק לפני בדור הזה
7.2	**Of every pure animal thou shalt take to thee seven and seven, <u>man and his wife</u>**; and of the **animals that are impure two and two, <u>man with his wife</u>**;	מכל הבהמה הטהורה תקח לך שבעה שבעה איש ואשתו ומן הבהמה אשר לא טהרה הוא שנים איש ואשתו
7.3	of the **bird of the air, seven and seven, <u>male and female;</u> to keep seed alive upon the face of all the earth.**	גם מעוף השמים שבעה שבעה זכר ונקבה לחיות זרע על פני כל הארץ
7.4	For in seven days, I will cause it to rain upon the earth forty days and forty nights; and I erase the entire universe that I have made off the face of the ground.'	כי לימים עוד שבעה אנכי ממטיר עלהארץ ארבעים יום וארבעים לילה ומחיתי את כל היקום אשר עשיתי מעל פני האדמה
7.5	**And Noah did according unto all that the Lord commanded him.**	ויעש נח ככל אשר צוהו יהוה
7.13	In the end of this day entered Noah, and Shem, and Ham, and Japheth, the sons of Noah, and Noah's wife, and the three	בעצם היום הזה בא נח ושם וחם ויפת בני נח ואשת נח ושלשת נשי בניו אתם אל התבה

	wives of his sons with them, into the ark;	
7.14	**they, and every beast to its kind**, and **all the cattle to its kind**, and **every creep that crawl upon the earth to its kind**, and **every bird after its kind, every bird every wing.**	המה וכל החיה למינה וכל הבהמה למינהו וכל הרמש הרמש על הארץ למינהו וכל העוף למינהו כל צפור כל כנף
7.15	And they went in unto Noah into the ark, two and two of **all the flesh that has live soul.**	ויבאו אל נח אל התבה שנים שנים מכל הבשר אשר בו רוח חיים
7.16	And they that went in, **went in male and female of all flesh, as God commanded him**; and the Lord shut him in.	והבאים זכר ונקבה מכל בשר באו כאשר צוה אתו אלהים ויסגר יהוה בעדו
7.20	Fifteen cubits upward did the waters prevail; and the mountains were covered.	חמש עשרה אמה מלמעלה גברו המים ויכסו ההרים
7.21	And **all flesh perished** that creep upon the earth, **birds**, and **cattle**, and **beast**, and **every swarming thing** that swarm upon the earth, **and every man**;	ויגוע כל בשר הרמש על הארץ בעוף ובבהמה ובחיה ובכל השרץ השרץ על הארץ וכל האדם
7.22	**all in whose nostrils were with breath of live soul, whatever was in the dry land, died.**	כל אשר נשמת רוח חיים באפיו מכל אשר בחרבה מתו
7.23	And He blotted out the universe	וימח את כל היקום אשר על פני

which was upon the face of the ground, from **man**, to **cattle**, and **creeping things**, and the **birds** of the sky; and **they were blotted out from the earth**; and Noah only was left, and they that were with him in the ark.

האדמה מאדם עד בהמה עד רמש ועד עוף השמים וימחו מן הארץ וישאר אך נח ואשר אתו בתבה

8.15 And **God spoke unto Noah, saying**:

וידבר אלהים אל נח לאמר

8.16 Go forth from the ark, thou, and thy wife, and thy sons, and thy sons' wives with thee.

צא מן התבה אתה ואשתך ובניך ונשי בניך אתך

8.17 **Bring forth with thee every animal** that is with thee **of all flesh**, the **birds**, and **cattle**, and **every creeping thing that creeps upon the earth**; that **they may swarm in the earth, and be fruitful, and multiply upon the earth.**'

כל החיה אשר אתך מכל בשר בעוף ובבהמה ובכל הרמש הרמש עלהארץ הוצא היצא אתך ושרצו בארץ ופרו ורבו עלהארץ

8.18 And Noah went forth, and his sons, and his wife, and his sons' wives with him;

ויצא נח ובניו ואשתו ונשי בניו אתו

8.19 every animal, every creep, and every bird, whatever crawl upon the earth, to their families; went out of the ark.

כל החיה כל הרמש וכל העוף כל רומש על הארץ למשפחתיהם יצאו מן התבה

8.20	**And Noah built an altar** unto the Lord; and **took of every clean animal, and of every clean bird, and offered burnt-offerings on the altar.**	ויבן נח מזבח ליהוה ויקח מכל הבהמה הטהורה ומכל העוף הטהר ויעל עלת במזבח
8.21	And **God smelled the scent**; and the **God said in His heart: 'I will not again curse the ground any more for man's sake; for the man's nature is evil from his youth; neither will I again smite any more living**, as I have done.	וירח יהוה את ריח הניחח ויאמר יהוה אל לבו לא אסף לקלל עוד את האדמה בעבור האדם כי יצר לב האדם רע מנעריו ולא אסף עוד להכות את כל חי כאשר עשיתי
8.22	While the earth remains seed time and harvest, and cold and heat, and summer and winter, and day and night shall not cease.'	עד כל ימי הארץ זרע וקציר וקר וחם וקיץ וחרף ויום ולילה לא ישבתו
9.1	And **God blessed Noah and his sons, and said unto them: 'Be fruitful and multiply, and replenish the earth**.	ויברך אלהים את נח ואת בניו ויאמר להם פרו ורבו ומלאו את הארץ
9.2	And **the fear of you and the dread of you shall be upon every beast of the earth, and upon every bird of the sky, upon all that creeps the ground, and upon all the fish	ומוראכם וחתכם יהיה על כל חית הארץ ועל כל עוף השמים בכל אשר תרמש האדמה ובכל דגי הים בידכם נתנו

	of the sea: <u>**in your hand are they given**</u>.	
9.3	**Every creep that lives shall be for you as food; as the green herb**, I have given you all.	כל רמש אשר הוא חי לכם יהיה לאכלה כירק עשב נתתי לכם את כל
9.4	**But flesh with a soul, its blood, shall ye not eat.**	אך בשר בנפשו דמו לא תאכלו
9.5	**And surely your blood of your souls will I require**; at the hand of every beast will I require it; and at the hand of man, even at the hand of every man's brother, will I require the life of man.	ואך את דמכם לנפשתיכם אדרש מיד כל חיה אדרשנו ומיד האדם מיד איש אחיו אדרש את נפש האדם
9.6	**Who so sheds man's blood, by man shall his blood be shed;** for in the image of God made man.	שפך דם האדם באדם דמו ישפך כי בצלם אלהים עשה את האדם
9.7	And you, be ye fruitful, and multiply; **swarm in the earth, and multiply** therein.'	ואתם פרו ורבו שרצו בארץ ורבובה
9.8	**And God spoke unto Noah, and to his sons with him, saying:**	ויאמר אלהים אל נח ואל בניו אתו לאמר
9.9	**I am here, establish My covenant with you, and with your seed after you;**	ואני הנני מקים את בריתי אתכם ואת זרעכם אחריכם
9.10	and <u>**with every living soul that**</u>	ואת כל נפש החיה אשר אתכם

	is with you, the bird, the **cattle**, and **every beast of the earth** with you; of all that go out of the ark, with every beast of the earth.	בעוף בבהמה ובכל חית הארץ אתכם מכל יצאי התבה לכל חית הארץ
9.11	And **I will establish My covenant with you; neither shall all flesh be cut off any more** by the waters of the flood; be a flood to destroy the earth.'neither shall there anymore	והקמתי את בריתי אתכם ולא יכרת כל בשר עוד ממי המבול ולא יהיה עוד מבול לשחת הארץ
9.12	And **God said: 'This is the sign of** the covenant which I make between Me and you <u>and every living creature</u> **that is with you, for perpetual generations**:	ויאמר אלהים זאת אות הברית אשר אני נתן ביני וביניכם ובין כל נפש חיה אשר אתכם לדרת עולם
9.13	I have set My bow in the cloud, and it shall be for a sign of a covenant between Me and the earth.	את קשתי נתתי בענן והיתה לאות ברית ביני ובין הארץ
9.14	And it shall come to pass, when I bring clouds over the earth, and the bow is seen in the cloud,	והיה בענני ענן על הארץ ונראתה הקשת בענן
9.15	that I will **remember My covenant**, which is **between Me**	וזכרתי את בריתי אשר ביני וביניכם ובין כל נפש חיה בכל

	and you <u>and every living creature of all flesh</u>; and the waters shall no more become a flood to destroy all flesh.	בשר ולא יהיה עוד המים למבול לשחת כל בשר
9.16	And **the bow shall be in the cloud**; and I will **look upon it**, that I may **remember the everlasting covenant** between God and every living creature **of all flesh that is upon the earth.'**	והיתה הקשת בענן וראיתיה לזכר ברית עולם בין אלהים ובין כל נפש חיה בכל בשר אשר על הארץ
9.17	And **God said unto Noah**: 'This is the sign of the **covenant** which **I have established between Me and all flesh that is upon the earth.'**	ויאמר אלהים אל נח זאת אות הברית אשר הקמתי ביני ובין כל בשר אשר על הארץ
9.18	And the sons of Noah, that went forth from the ark, were Shem, and Ham, and Japheth; and Ham is the father of Canaan.	ויהיו בני נח היצאים מן התבה שם וחם ויפת וחם הוא אבי כנען

God chose Noah, the most righteous man out of his whole generation, who followed his way. God ordered him to build an ark and gather every living soul; Noah and his wife, sons and their wives, animals, birds, creeps, crawlers and wild beasts into the ark to preserve his creations in their original nature, as it was before the earth went violent and corrupt. The era when every animal, bird, creep, beast and mankind had the recipe from God in a divine providence. God gathered the different kinds of **living souls** and **all flesh** and brought them into the ark. Verse after verse, we are witnessing the importance God places on all types of living creatures.

You'll see in Verse 7.2 that the words איש ואישתו are used when referring to animals (both pure and impure - normally translated as clean and unclean). איש ואישתו are normally translated as "each and his mate" but it actually says "man and his wife" which are words that are normally used when speaking about humans. In fact, in Verse 7.3, immediately after, the words זכר ונקבה are used, which mean "male and female". Given that The Bible is perfect and there are no mistakes in this holy book, this wording is intentional. There is no distinction made between any of God creations; human and its partner or any other creature and its mate.

7.2	Of every pure animal thou shalt take to thee seven and seven, **man and his wife**; and of the **animals that are impure** two and two, **man with his wife**;	מכל הבהמה הטהורה תקח לך שבעה שבעה **איש ואשתו** ומן הבהמה אשר לא טהרה הוא שנים **איש ואשתו**
7.3	of the **bird of the air, seven and seven, male and female;** to keep seed alive upon the face of all the earth.	גם מעוף השמים שבעה שבעה זכר ונקבה לחיות זרע על פני כל הארץ

There are many instances where common language and repetition of a phrase is used to describe mankind as well as other creatures prompting us to dig deeper into the meaning. For example in 7.21 the phrase "swarm upon the earth" is used to describe creatures besides mankind and in 9.7 it is used as a command from God *to* mankind.

7.21	And **all flesh perished** that creep upon the earth, **birds**, and **cattle**, and **beast**, and **every swarming thing** that swarm upon the earth, **and every man**;	ויגוע כל בשר הרמש על הארץ בעוף ובבהמה ובחיה ובכל השרץ השרץ על הארץ וכל האדם
9.7	And you, be ye fruitful, and multiply; **swarm in the earth, and multiply** therein.'	ואתם פרו ורבו שרצו בארץ ורבובה

God is calling all his living soul creations in the word; **Flesh**

7.21	And **all flesh** perished that creep upon the earth, birds, and cattle, and beast, and every swarming thing that swarm upon the earth, and every man;	ויגוע כל בשר הרמש על הארץ בעוף ובבהמה ובחיה ובכל השרץ השרץ על הארץ וכל האדם
7.22	all in whose nostrils were with breath of live spirit soul, whatever was in the dry land, died.	כל אשר נשמת רוח חיים באפיו מכל אשר בחרבה מתו

Mankind is clearly above the animals, but we were never commanded by God to use them as burnt-offerings on the altar. When God tells Noah to go out of the ark after the flood, he is sure that Noah and his wife, his sons and wives, are going to recreate mankind as they were intended to be in the authentic creation, since Noah was the most righteous and innocent in his generation.

8.15	And God spoke unto Noah, saying:	וידבר אלהים אל נח לאמר
8.16	Go forth from the ark, thou, and thy wife, and thy sons, and thy sons' wives with thee.	צא מן התבה אתה ואשתך ובניך ונשי בניך אתך
8.17	Bring forth with thee every animal that is with thee of all flesh, the birds, and cattle, and every creeping thing that creep upon the earth; that they may swarm in the earth, and be fruitful, and multiply upon the earth.'	כל החיה אשר אתך מכל בשר בעוף ובבהמה ובכל הרמש הרמש על הארץ הוצא היצא אתך ושרצו בארץ ופרו ורבו על הארץ

But this did not happen. Instead of doing good in the eyes of the Lord, Noah chose violence by sacrificing one of the living souls God had just entrusted to him. This type of violence is what caused the flood and erased the entire flesh on earth in the first place. Through violent sacrifice, he went back to the ways of paganism.

| 8.20 | And Noah built an altar unto the Lord; and took of every clean | ויבן נח מזבח ליהוה ויקח מכל הבהמה הטהורה ומכל העוף הטהר ויעל עלת במזבח |

> animal, and of every clean bird, and offered burnt-offerings on the altar.

God had smelled the scent of a burnt animal and thought in his heart; After all the effort of trying to reconstruct the world, he realized it would not change because of the evil nature of mankind's heart. Instead of taking a step towards purity, Noah had gone back to the ways that brought the flesh eliminating flood.

> **8.21** And God smelled the scent; and the God said in His heart: 'I will not again curse the ground any more for man's sake; for the man's nature is evil from his youth; neither will I again smite any more living, as I have done.
>
> וירח יהוה את ריח הניחח ויאמר יהוה אל לבו לא אסף לקלל עוד את האדמה בעבור האדם כי יצר לב האדם רע מנעריו ולא אסף עוד להכות את כל חי כאשר עשיתי

Then, God is Blessing all seeds and harvest, cold and heat, summer and winter forever to revive nature.

> **8.22** While the earth remains seed time and harvest, and cold and heat, and summer and winter, and day and night shall not cease.'
>
> עד כל ימי הארץ זרע וקציר וקר וחם וקיץ וחרף ויום ולילה לא ישבתו

Blessing Noah's family with fertility for generations to come and placing mankind above all animals of earth, birds of the sky, creeps of the ground and fish of the sea. God gave us the blessing and responsibility to care for the animals. The fear and dread that the animals should have under us is the same kind we have under God and children often feel under their parents.

9.1	And God blessed Noah and his sons, and said unto them: 'Be fruitful and multiply, and replenish the earth.	ויברך אלהים את נח ואת בניו ויאמר להם פרו ורבו ומלאו את הארץ
9.2	And the fear of you and the dread of you shall be upon every beast of the earth, and upon every bird of the sky, upon all that creeps the ground, and upon all the fish of the sea: in your hand are they given.	ומוראכם וחתכם יהיה על כל חית הארץ ועל כל עוף השמים בכל אשר תרמש האדמה ובכל דגי הים בידכם נתנו

The following passage is often used to justify eating flesh but it is nearly always mistranslated. In this passage God is instructing Noah on what will be his food. In Most books, the translation for the Hebrew word REMES רמש, is "every moving thing." Subsequently, people have allowed themselves to eat every moving thing. The actual meaning of the word is "creep", as in the smallest animal (including insects) that were looking as if they are crawling on the ground, like Locust.

9.3	Every creep that lives shall be	כל רמש אשר הוא חי לכם יהיה

for you as food; as the green herb, I have given you all.	לאכלה כירק עשב נתתי לכם את כל

God is promising, like vegetation herbs, I gave you all. Sages say, it is a punishment for killing the flesh that God himself had created. Then, God continues and says;

But flesh with soul, you will not eat.

Blood is often referring to a soul, like the phrase "spilling someone's blood," which means murdering someone. There are further passages which say that a man murdering a live soul animal is equivalent to a man murdering man - both murderers' souls will be claimed.

This next verse is one of the most important verses, where mistranslation resulted in the world we experience today.

9.4	אך בשר בנפשו דמו לא תאכלו

"you must not, however, eat flesh with its life-blood in it"
(English translation for the Torah)

"but flesh with the life thereof, which is the blood thereof, shall you not eat"
(King James translation of Old Testament)

According to most Bible versions this verse is teaching that when eating flesh, the blood is forbidden as food, as it represent the life of the soul. However, the way this sentence was translated is too basic and clearly done out of convenience. Every word was translated separately and, in doing so, the meaning was completely lost.

When translating from the ancient Hebrew scrolls, many factors need to be considered. In many instances words can not be translated one by one because the complete phrase has a different meaning from the words separately. This is even more critical in this case, since the original Hebrew texts are also lacking punctuation and vowels. Translating word by word without reflection on context can and does result in several entirely different translations. Word combinations appear to look the same, but construct a much different meaning. The follows translations by the sages uncover the true meaning of the same verse.

9.4 But Soul with Flesh, its blood, you shall not eat

Ancient Hebrew is a complex language that requires a sophisticated translation technique. Superficial word by word translations loses the original meaning. The Hebrew language has incredible depth and every letter, word, number, sentence and story has more than one meaning.

In the beginning, Adam was made pure and the only food for him was fruits and vegetables; nothing he ate was the result of violence. Throughout our history, God has consistently hinted and directed his followers and worshipers towards purity. Over and over we see God say that we are not to butcher or murder his creations (all flesh). Despite clever punctuation this sentence can never mean we are permitted to eat flesh.

Blood, is the life of the soul. Without blood, the body does not function and the soul has no life in it. When using the phrase; 'spill someone's blood', the meaning is 'murdering someone'. Eating the blood, is worse than spilling the blood. Not only is there a murder, but there is a consumption of the body and soul.

> **9.4** **But Flesh in his soul, its blood you shall not destroy (Sages)**

Many Hebrew words have more than one meaning although they look very similar. Sometimes, these words are constructed of the same letters. Punctuation assists in reading and understanding. Individual words and sentences are better understood through context by reading the story from the beginning to the end. The words and sentences from The Bible can be discussed for hours and days. Words are very important for understanding and grasping the real meaning of every verse.

For example, the Hebrew word אכל **'AKHAL'** often translated as "food" has other more powerful meanings that indicate the path God wants mankind to follow. The word also means to consume as in to destroy. This word is also used as a root In other words like **מאכלת,** which means **Butchering Knife**. Below is the the same word אכל which has many meanings based on the vowel marks used (and remember there were no vowels in the ancient texts). Even in Modern Hebrew, the vowel marks are not normally included and the meaning is made through the context of the sentence.

אָכַל
to eat ; to destroy, to consume
אֹכֶל
food ; dining, meal
אֻכַּל
to be consumed, to be destroyed
אִכֵּל
to consume, destroy

So, what does the verse say about God's creation?

9:4 Flesh in its soul, its life, you shall not destroy!
9:4 Flesh in its soul, its life, you shall not consume!

Meaning:
Nobody can murder a soul, especially for food!
God does not allow anyone and has never given the authorization to
Murder his creations.
The text was taken and translated incorrectly and irresponsibly, for
mankind's evil use and wicked ways of living.
There are many passages in The Bible where אכל is translated as
destroy/consume. One example comes from Exodus:

Exodus 32:10
New American Standard Bible
"Now then let Me alone, that My anger may burn against them and that I may **destroy** them; and I will make of you a great nation."

King James Bible
Now therefore let me alone, that my wrath may wax hot against them, and that I may **consume** them: and I will make of thee a great nation.

ועתה הניחה לי ויחר־אפי בהם ואכלם ואעשה אותך לגוי גדול

You can begin to see how the translator controls the meaning and therefore is able to lead the reader to the conclusion they want.

9.4 | But Flesh as exchange to his soul, you shall not eat (Sages)

Another important example is the Hebrew word דמו 'DAMO', which is translated as **"Its Blood"** The word also has other meanings that greatly change the meaning of the sentence it is in.
דמו 'DAMO', 'DAMAV'; **"Its Price"**, as well as **"Its Return / Its exchange"** - תמורה

What does the verse say about God's creation?

9:4 Soul that was paid for its flesh, shall not be eaten!

Meaning:
Nobody can **Buy a murdered soul,** for **food!**

Again we see that God has not given us permission to Murder his creations (especially not for food). These texts were translated by people who lived in a culture where eating flesh was the norm and therefore translated the text to suit their lifestyle. It is not what was intended and not what it says in the original.

Importantly, the verse that comes immediately after talks about the punishment for murdering God's creations for food, buying a murdered soul for its flesh, or eating a soul's flesh blood. Something to keep in mind is that, again, there was no punctuation so there were also no verses. The separations between sentences and sentence groups were done by modern translators. This passage clearly follows the directive God gave to not eat flesh and outlines the consequences for doing so.

| 9.5 | **And surely your blood of your souls will I require**; at the hand of every beast will I require it; and at the hand of man, even at the hand of every man's brother, will I require the life of man. | ואך את דמכם לנפשתיכם אדרש מיד כל חיה אדרשנו ומיד האדם מיד איש אחיו אדרש את נפש האדם |

This entire passage, when read as one unit the way it is in the original text, says:

But Flesh as exchange to his soul, you shall not eat and surely your blood of your souls will I require; at the hand of every beast will I require it; and at the hand of man, even at the hand of every man's brother, will I require the life of man.

The meaning is clear:
God will require the life of mankind's souls if they eat flesh (meat).

The verse continues, saying:

9.6	Who so sheds man's blood, by man shall his blood be shed; for in the image of God made man.	שפך דם האדם באדם דמו ישפך כי בצלם אלהים עשה את האדם

Then God makes a covenant with all living creatures, all living souls, **all flesh** that were in the ark.

9.8	And God spoke unto Noah, and to his sons with him, saying:	ויאמר אלהים אל נח ואל בניו אתו לאמר
9.9	I am here, establish My covenant with you, and with your seed after you;	ואני הנני מקים את בריתי אתכם ואת זרעכם אחריכם
9.10	and with every living soul that is with you, the bird, the cattle, and every beast of the earth with you; of all that go out of the ark, with every beast of the earth.	ואת כל נפש החיה אשר אתכם בעוף בבהמה ובכל חית הארץ אתכם מכל יצאי התבה לכל חית הארץ
9.11	And I will establish My covenant with you; neither shall all flesh be cut off any more by the waters of the flood; neither shall there anymore be a flood to destroy the earth.'	והקמתי את בריתי אתכם ולא יכרת כל בשר עוד ממי המבול ולא יהיה עוד מבול לשחת הארץ
9.12	And God said: 'This is the sign of the covenant which I make between Me and you and every living creature that is with you,	ויאמר אלהים זאת אות הברית אשר אני נתן ביני וביניכם ובין כל נפש חיה אשר אתכם לדרת עולם

for perpetual generations:

Remember the sign of God's covenant with every living creature.
When you see it, you will remember, forever!

9.13	I have set My bow in the cloud, and it shall be for a sign of a covenant between Me and the earth.	את קשתי נתתי בענן והיתה לאות ברית ביני ובין הארץ
9.14	And it shall come to pass, when I bring clouds over the earth, and the bow is seen in the cloud,	והיה בענני ענן על הארץ ונראתה הקשת בענן
9.17	And God said unto Noah: 'This is the sign of the covenant which I have established between Me and all flesh that is upon the earth.'	ויאמר אלהים אל נח זאת אות הברית אשר הקמתי ביני ובין כל בשר אשר על הארץ

God's covenant is between him and all Flesh.
The divine covenant between God and all and every Flesh for eternity is repeated again and again throughout these verses. The Hebrew word **בשר** 'Basar' which is translated as "Flesh", has another meaning that was used in biblical days and is still used in Modern Hebrew; Meat.

Meat is the material that surrounds the bones and makes a living body. Mankind, Animals, Cattle and Birds are all meat and flesh. Mankind are humans. Animals are the wild beasts. Cattle are the grass eaters. Birds are the avian dinosaurs and winged creatures.

Chapter 7

Solomon's Wisdom

King Solomon was King of Israel, following the death of his father, King David and was responsible for the building of the First Jewish Temple in Jerusalem. He is considered one of the 48 prophets and is credited with writing, Book of Proverbs, Ecclesiastes, and Song of Songs. His legend includes having incredible wisdom, which greatly influenced Judaism, Christianity and Islam.

The following excerpts from Proverbs, written by King Solomon (Shlomoh), are all about morality, wisdom, and justice.

Proverb 1

2	To know wisdom and morality; to comprehend the words of wisdom;	ב לדעת חכמה ומוסר להבין אמרי בינה.
3	To receive the discipline of wisdom, justice, and right, and equity;	ג לקחת מוסר השכל צדק ומשפט ומישרים
10	My son, if sins entice you, do not consent.	י בני אם־יפתוך חטאים אל־תבא
11	If they say: 'Come with us,	יא אם־יאמרו לכה אתנו נארבה לדם נצפנה לנקי חנם

	let us lie in wait for blood, let us lurk for the innocent without cause	
15	My son, do not walk in their way, restrain your foot from their path;	טו בני אל־תלך בדרך אתם מנע רגלך מנתיבתם
16	For their feet run to evil, and they make haste to shed blood.	טז כי רגליהם לרע ירוצו וימהרו לשפך־דם
17	For in vain the net is spread in the eyes of any bird;	יז כי־חנם מזרה הרשת בעיני כל־בעל כנף
18	And they ambush for their own blood, they lurk for the souls.	יח והם לדמם יארבו יצפנו לנפשתם
19	So are the ways of every one that is greedy of gain; it takes away the life of its owners.	יט כן ארחות כל־בצע בצע את־נפש בעליו יקח
31	Therefore shall they eat of the fruit of their own way, and be filled with their own advice.	לא ויאכלו מפרי דרכם וממעצתיהם ישבעו
32	For the way of the naive shall kill them, and the confidence of fools shall destroy them.	לב כי משובת פתים תהרגם ושלות כסילים תאבדם
33	And whom listens to me shall live securely, and shall	לג ושמע לי ישכן־בטח ושאנן מפחד רעה

> **be serene without fear of evil.**

The wisdom within this proverb should awaken your morality and, when it does, your actions will change accordingly. Once the veil has been lifted you will not be easily enticed by sins, not yours, not others. Knowing God's original intentions you'll avoid any chance of, invitation by others or your own desire to go and hunt innocent souls. You'll also obviously avoid killing an animal without a justified cause, such as mercy killing due to a illness or severe injury. Taking the blood is taking the soul of flesh. And as we have seen, it is forbidden to do so, by the divine law.

When greed becomes a way of life, it takes a toll not just on the victim but on the mind of the one who chooses to live that way too. This way of life becomes natural and we convince ourselves that this way is normal and it becomes our reality. For the people who hold this way of life, it is very hard to see through the veil and make changes. For those who were born into this way of life and are totally unaware, illness and disease often result and cause pain, suffering, and even death. The ones who are aware of this way being wrong and ignore it out of comfort, will be lost forever and that will impact them both physically and spiritually.

"He who becomes compassionate to the cruel will ultimately become cruel to the compassionate" (Sages)

Whoever comes back to the way God intended us to live, will live in serenity and without fear.

Proverb 4

| 13 | Take fast hold of morality, do not let her go; keep her, for she | יג החזק במוסר אל־תרף נצרה כי־היא חייך |

	is your life.	
14	Enter not into the path of the wicked, and walk not in the way of evil men.	יד בארח רשעים אל־תבא ואל־תאשר בדרך רעים
15	Avoid it, pass not by it; turn from it, and pass on.	טו פרעהו אל־תעבר־בו שטה מעליו ועבור
16	For they sleep not, except they have done evil; and their sleep is taken away, unless they cause some to fall.	טז כי לא ישנו אם־לא ירעו ונגזלה נתם אם לא יכשולו
17	For they eat the bread of wickedness, and drink the wine of violence	יז כי לחמו לחם רשע ויין חמסים ישתו
18	And the path of the righteous is as the light of dawn, that shines more and more unto the perfect day.	יח וארח צדיקים כאור נגה הולך ואור עד־נכון היום

13 Hold and never let go of Morality, cherish it for it is the way your life keeps to the right and healthy route.

14 Do not connect your heart and mind with cruel people.

15 Do not make it the way you live. Do not approve nor go in the wrong and cruel way. If you are feeling pressured to live a certain way by society's influence, remind yourself of your morality, discharge the burden, and do not walk the path of evil. Sadly you may find that some treat you as crazy or a fool, but move on and continue to improve your ways.

16 If unkind people will keep their unpleasant way, they will not sleep well.

17 They are fed on evil and drunk on violence.

18 When choosing the righteous way, life shines on you.

Proverb 6

16	There are six things which God hated, yea, seven which are an abomination unto His Soul:	טז שש־הנה שנא יהוה ושבע תועבת נפשו
17	Haughty eyes, a lying tongue, and hands that shed innocent blood;	יז עינים רמות לשון שקר וידים שפכות דם־נקי
18	A heart that devise wicked thoughts, feet that are swift in running to evil;	יח לב חרש מחשבות און רגלים ממהרות לרוץ לרעה
19	A false witness that breathe out lies, and he that sowed discord among brethren.	יט יפיח כזבים עד שקר ומשלח מדנים בין אחים

Sins despised by God
- Looking at others from above, arrogance
- Lying to create a situation that will support a standpoint
- Shedding innocent blood directly and indirectly
- Changing a view in a heartbeat and running towards negativity
- Telling lies
- Creating conflicts between people

Proverb 8

35	For whom finds me finds life, and obtained favor of God	לה כי מצאי חיים ויפק רצון מיהוה
36	But he that misses me, wrong his own soul; all they that hate me love death	לו וחטאי חמס נפשו כל־משנאי אהבו מות

35 Whomever finds me in their life, finds the will of life

Whomever finds God, loves life and cares about all living creatures, all God's creations.

36 Whomever misses me, destroys his own soul with violence. Whomever hates me, loves Death. Whomever does not care about the life of others, whether mankind or wild or domesticated creatures of nature, and supports their death willfully or through ignorance, obviously hates God since they support the death of his creations.

Proverb 11

| 17 | The merciful man does good to his own soul; but he that is cruel troubles his own glow. | יז גמל נפשו איש חסד ועכר ארו אכזרי |

18	The wicked earned deceitful wages; but he that sowed righteousness hath a sure reward.	יח רשע עשה פעלת־שקר וזרע צדקה שכר אמת

17 Rewards his soul - Compassionate man
Corrupts himself - Evil person

18 Evil person - does False activities
Righteous person - awarded truly

Proverb 12

9	Love morality, love knowledge and despise the reproofs of the ignorant	אהב מוסר אהב דעת ושנא תוכחת בער
10	A righteous recognizes the soul in an animal; Those who show mercy to the evil are cruel.	י יודע צדיק נפש בהמתו ורחמי רשעים אכזרי
11	He who works his ground shall have plenty of bread; but he who follows vain things is void of heart	יא עבד אדמתו ישבע־לחם ומרדף ריקים חסר־לב
12	The wicked desires the prey of evil; but the root of the righteous yield fruit	יב חמד רשע מצוד רעים ושרש צדיקים יתן

9 Love, connect and follow morality and knowledge and despise reproofing of ignorance

10 The righteous knows his animal's feelings and needs. When pitying and forgiving evil deeds, you are cruel.

Ignoring the sorrow of the animals and seeing them as only for the "needs" of mankind, is heartless and wrong in the eyes of God.

11 One who works the land, gains bread satiation.

One who chases emptiness, loses his heart.

Working for things, will bring results and satisfaction.

Following an empty cause, will lead you nowhere.

12 The lust of the wicked hunts for evil.

The seed of righteousness will be given to the those who do good.

Creatures, souls of the wild and domesticated ones, are exploited, tested and experimented on, and hunted for their flesh (meat), fur, skin, bones or other parts. Sometimes for the hunter's personal delight. **The fruit of roots, does not bring grief to souls.**

Chapter 8

The Sin of Lust

Since Noah's days, when God said mankind was born with evil, God has taken a different approach and now communicates to us through warnings and appeals, rather than destruction and force.

Deuteronomy 12

God has given you land and widened your borders as he promised you, then yet you say, I will eat meat, because your soul has lust, you shall eat it with your lust, therefore the place where God puts his name will be far and farther away from you. Then, sacrifice and eat in your own home with all your soul's lust. (And not before god, as god commands)!!! If you eat the flesh of deer and gazelle, eat the sick parts with the healthy, but please, be strong enough not to eat the blood, for it is the soul. You will not eat it for it will be better for you and your sons after you, for you will do the good in the eyes of god. Only your holiness and vows shall you carry and go to the place where god commanded you. Your sacrifices of flesh and blood; the blood will spill on the altar and the flesh will be eaten by the fire. Keep all my commandments for it will be better for you and your sons after you until forever. Beware of following other gods. The gentiles used to sacrifice in fire any flesh including their own sons and daughters.
Do everything I command

Not more
Not less

Eating meat/flesh, in the eyes of God, is the wrong thing to do.
Since the day Adam ate from the Tree of Knowledge mankind has had the freedom to choose between good and bad, right and wrong. God's tone, is a mixture of commands and pleas, since we can choose our way.

God's words
" I have given you more land as I have promised and Yet, you are asking to eat meat/flesh because of your Lust for it."

Every time you eat meat, God will put his name farther and farther away from you. If you choose to eat meat, you shall eat it with all your Lust. Eat the sick parts with the healthy but please, try to be strong enough and get over your lust for blood, do not eat the blood, for it is the creation's soul. If you do not eat Flesh, you and your descendants will have a better future forever.

Only your holiness and vows shall you carry and go to the place where god commanded you.

Your sacrifice, flesh and blood; the blood will spill on the altar; the flesh will be eaten by the fire

Keep all my commandments
Do not do more
Do not do less

כי ירחיב יהוה אלהיך את גבלך כאשר דבר לך ואמרת אכלה בשר **כי תאוה נפשך לאכל בשר**
בכל אות נפשך תאכל בשר כי ירחק ממך המקום אשר יבחר יהוה אלהיך לשום שמו שם
וזבחת מבקרך ומצאנך אשר נתן יהוה לך כאשר צויתך ואכלת בשעריך בכל אות נפשך
אך כאשר יאכל את הצבי ואת האיל כן תאכלנו הטמא והטהור יחדו יאכלנו
רק חזק לבלתי אכל הדם כי הדם הוא הנפש ולא תאכל הנפש עם הבשר
לא תאכלנו על הארץ תשפכנו כמים

לא תאכלנו למען ייטב לך ולבניך אחריך כי תעשה הישר בעיני יהוה

רק קדשיך אשר יהיו לך ונדריך תשא ובאת אל המקום אשר יבחר יהוה ועשית עלתיך

הבשר והדם על מזבח יהוה אלהיך ודם זבחיך ישפך על מזבח יהוה אלהיך והבשר תאכל

שמר ושמעת את כל הדברים האלה אשר אנכי מצוך למען ייטב לך ולבניך אחריך עד עולם כי תעשה הטוב והישר בעיני יהוה אלהיך

כי יכרית יהוה אלהיך את הגוים אשר אתה בא שמה לרשת אותם מפניך וירשת אתם וישבת בארצם

השמר לך פן תנקש אחריהם אחרי השמדם מפניך ופן תדרש לאלהיהם לאמר איכה יעבדו הגוים האלה את אלהיהם ואעשה כן גם אני

לא תעשה כן ליהוה אלהיך כי כל תועבת יהוה אשר שנא עשו לאלהיהם כי גם את בניהם ואת בנתיהם ישרפו באש לאלהיהם

את כל הדבר אשר אנכי מצוה אתכם אתו תשמרו לעשות לא תסף עליו ולא תגרע ממנו

Numbers 11: 33-44

And while the flesh was yet between their teeth, ere it was chewed, the wrath of the LORD was kindled against the people, and the LORD smote the people with a very great plague.

And he called the name of that place Kivrot ha'ta'avah (Graves of Lust): because there they buried the people that lusted.

הבשר עודנו בין שניהם טרם יכרת ואף יהוה חרה בעם ויך יהוה בעם מכה רבה מאד ויקרא את שם המקום ההוא קברות התאוה כי שם קברו את העם המתאוים

Chapter 9

The 6th Commandment

In Biblical days the ancient Israelites were given permission by God to kill other humans under very specific circumstances, such as punishment for murder, adultery, paganism or self defence. God also allowed the Israelites to engage in warfare according to his specific instructions.

In many books the 6th commandment is translated as "Thou shall not kill". Most of the translators and commentators also add, it concerns humans only and not animals when, as a matter of a fact the exact translation is "Do Not Murder" and it is not speaking specifically about humans murdering humans, but a very strict and clear prohibition of intentionally killing anything. One must agree that God did not intend his followers around the world to enslave and use animals in a way that is perverse beyond the all imagination. Murdering the innocent in modern days for mankind's use and convenience, is completely against God and human morals and values.

Open your mind to the real nature of this commandment and step out of your daily way of life and thinking. Are we fulfilling the 6 commandment? When directly or indirectly (through our consumer choices) we cause billions of innocent creatures to be brought into this world simply to leave this world by our hands we have broken the 6th commandment. The list of animals we use and abuse on a daily basis would fill a book, from the clothing we wear, to the food we eat, to things we think of as fun animals are suffering and being murdered for us as a result of our choices making us responsible. Disconnecting yourself mentally from the process involved in the things you buy and do does not absolve of your sin.

Being ignorant to the inherent and common abuse and torture that is daily business in many of the countries our goods come from does not release us from responsibility for it. Even in North America there is shocking barbarity for fashion such as the Canadian Seal hunt where hundreds of thousands of helpless baby seals are brutally murdered by being clubbed on the head. In Japan, Denmark and Greenland every year the waters turn red as tens of thousands of dolphins and whales are ritually and brutally murdered. Ripping the fur and skin off of Dogs, Cats, Raccoon Dogs, Fox, Wolves and many other animals while they are alive and many more inhumane methods of murder occur daily around the world.

It is against God
It is against any existing moral
It is against any existing value
Numbers 11, 22
Shall flocks and herds be slaughtered for them, and be enough for them? Or shall all the fish of the sea be gathered together for them, and be enough for them?

הצאן ובקר ישחט להם ומצא להם אם את־כל־דגי הים יאסף להם ומצא להם

Mankind should reconsider its role and the consequences of its actions on God's creations. We should all take steps towards returning to purity, the way God created us all.

God was very clear, during creation, what we were meant to eat. There is no ambiguity at all.

Genesis 1:29-30

And God Says:

Here, I give you all seed-bearing herb that is upon all the earth and every seed-bearing fruit tree, will be for you to eat.

And for every earth animal and for every bird of the sky and every creep that is upon the earth, which have a live soul in them, all vegetable herbs will be for food.

And God saw all that he has done and it was very good

ויאמר אלהים הנה נתתי לכם את־כל־עשב זרע זרע אשר על־פני כל־הארץ ואת־כל־העץ אשר־בו פרי־עץ זרע זרע לכם יהיה לאכלה
ולכל־חית הארץ ולכל־עוף השמים ולכל רומש על־הארץ אשר־בו נפש חיה את־כל־ירק עשב לאכלה ויהי־כן

Cain and Abel

Cain was a worker of the land.

Hevel (Abel) was a herder.

Cain brought God a vegetarian offering, unlike his brother who brought an offering from his flock.

God went towards Hevel's offering, but not to Cain's.

Why???

Why did God do it?

Are we content with a simple word by word reading and superficial interpretation (ie God went towards the meat offering not the vegetarian so therefore God approves of us murdering animals)?

The story continues with Cain then sinning by Killing his brother. Killing out of anger but not on purpose.

As we established, The Bible makes a distinction between the words "kill - הרג" and "murder - רצח" and it was written with such accuracy that it is hard to miss the true meaning, unless you are doing so for your own convenience.

Murder is killing intentionally
Kill is killing unintentionally.

God could have easily punished Cain with death, but he did not. God spared his life.
The one who served a meat offering ended up dead.
The one who served a vegetarian offering lived.
He was punished for his kill and yet he lived!

Chapter 10

Sorrow of the animal as the sorrow of mankind

This chapter highlights some of the verses in The Bible that show clearly how we are intended to treat animals. These are a few examples where The Bible gives rules that favor an animal's welfare.

Exodus 23, 4
If you meet your enemy's ox or his donkey going astray, you shall bring it back to him

כי תפגע שור איבך או חמרו תעה השב תשיבנו לו

Exodus 23, 5
Whenever you see that the donkey of someone who hates you has collapsed under its load, don't leave it there. Be sure to help him with his animal.

כי־תראה חמור שנאך רבץ תחת משאו וחדלת מעזב לו עזב תעזב עמו

Exodus 23, 7
Stay far away from a false accusation. Do not kill the innocent and the just, because I will not justify the cruelty.

מדבר־שקר תרחק ונקי וצדיק אל־תהרג כי לא־אצדיק רשע

Exodus 23, 11

but let the land be renewed and lie uncultivated during the seventh year. Then let the poor among you harvest whatever grows on its own. Leave the rest for wild animals to eat. The same applies to your vineyards and olive groves.

והשביעת תשמטנה ונטשתה ואכלו אביני עמך ויתרם תאכל חית השדה כן־תעשה לכרמך לזיתך

Exodus 23, 12

Six days do your work, but on the seventh day do not work, so that your ox and your donkey may rest

ששת ימים תעשה מעשיך וביום השביעי תשבת למען ינוח שורך וחמרך

Exodus 23, 19

You are to bring the best of the first fruits of your soil to the house of the LORD your God. You are not to boil a young goat in its mother's milk.

ראשית בכורי אדמתך תביא בית יהוה אלהיך לא־תבשל גדי בחלב אמו

Exodus 22, 30-31

Likewise shalt thou do with thine oxen, and with thy sheep; seven days it shall be with its dam; on the eighth day thou shalt give it Me.

And ye shall be holy men unto Me; therefore ye shall not eat any flesh that is of beasts in the field; ye shall cast it to the dogs.

כן־תעשה לשרך לצאנך שבעת ימים יהיה עם־אמו ביום השמיני תתנו־לי ואנשי־קדש תהיון לי ובשר בשדה טרפה לא תאכלו לכלב תשלכון אתו

Deutoronomy 22, 1-2

You shall not see your countryman's ox or his sheep straying away, and pay no attention to them; you shall certainly bring them back to your countryman. If your countryman is not near you, or if you do not know him, then you shall bring it home to your house, and it shall remain with you until your countryman looks for it; then you shall restore it to him.

לא־תראה את־שור אחיך או את־שיו נדחים והתעלמת מהם השב תשיבם לאחיך ואם־לא קרוב אחיך אליך ולא ידעתו ואספתו אל־תוך ביתך והיה עמך עד דרש אחיך אתו והשבתו לו

Deutoronomy 22, 4

You shall not see your countryman's donkey or his ox fallen down on the way, and pay no attention to them; you shall certainly help him to raise them up.

לא־תראה את־חמור אחיך או שורו נפלים בדרך והתעלמת מהם הקם תקים עמו

Deutoronomy 25, 4

Do not muzzle an ox while it treads out grain

לא־תחסם שור בדישו

Deutoronomy 22, 10

Do not plow with an ox and a donkey together.

לא־תחרש בשור־ובחמר יחדו

Exodus 22, 19

Whoever has sexual intercourse with an animal must be put to death

כל שכב עם בהמה מות יומת

Genesis 9, 4
Soul that was paid for its flesh
shall not be eaten
Flesh in its soul, its life, you shall not destruct

Chapter 11

Recipe of Health

In every instance in The Bible where vegetation, grains, beans, fruit and other plant based food are mentioned, they are always in the context of good health and cleanliness.

Daniel 1, 12-13
Please test your servants for 10 days. Let us be given vegetables to eat and water to drink

נס־נא את־עבדיך ימים עשרה ויתנו־לנו מן־הזרעים ונאכלה ומים ונשתה

Then examine our appearance and the appearance of the young men who are eating the king's food, and deal with your servants based on what you see

ויראו לפניך מראינו ומראה הילדים האכלים את פתבג המלך וכאשר תראה עשה עם־עבדיך

Ezekiel 4, 9
Take wheat and barley, beans and lentils, millet and spelt; put them in a storage jar and use them to make bread for yourself. You are to eat it during the 390 days you lie on your side

ואתה קח־לך חטין ושערים ופול ועדשים ודחן וכסמים ונתתה אותם בכלי אחד ועשית אותם לך ללחם מספר הימים אשר־אתה | שוכב על־צדך שלש־מאות ותשעים יום תאכלנו

Genesis 3, 19
By the sweat of your face you shall eat bread, till you return to the ground, for out of it you were taken; for you are dust, and to dust you shall return

בזעת אפיך תאכל לחם עד שובך אל־האדמה כי ממנה לקחת כי־עפר אתה ואל־עפר תשוב

Deuteronomy 8, 7-8
For the LORD your God is bringing you into a good land, a land of brooks of water, of fountains and springs, flowing out in the valleys and hills, a land of wheat and barley, of vines and fig trees and pomegranates, a land of olive trees and honey

כי יהוה אלהיך מביאך אל־ארץ טובה ארץ נחלי מים עינת ותהמת יצאים בבקעה ובהר ארץ חטה ושערה וגפן ותאנה ורמון ארץ־זית שמן ודבש

Job 30, 4
they pick salt wort and the leaves of bushes, and the roots of the broom tree for their food

הקטפים מלוח עלי־שיח ושרש רתמים לחמם

Exodus 23, 25
But you shall serve the LORD your God, and He will bless
your bread and your water and remove illnesses from you.
ועבדתם את יהוה אלהיכם וברך את־לחמך ואת־מימיך והסרתי מחלה מקרבך

Chapter 12

The Rapture – End of days

When The Bible discusses what the world will be like when The Rapture happens, it describes a world much like the original Garden of Eden where all of God's creatures lived in harmony.

Isaiah 11, 6-10
In that day, the wolf and the lamb will live together; the leopard will lie down with the baby goat. The calf and the yearling will be safe with the lion, and a little child will lead them all

וגר זאב עם־כבש ונמר עם־גדי ירבץ ועגל וכפיר ומריא יחדו ונער קטן נהג בם

The cow will graze near the bear. The cub and the calf will lie down together. The lion will eat hay like a cow.

ופרה ודב תרעינה יחדו ירבצו ילדיהן ואריה כבקר יאכל־תבן

The baby will play safely near the hole of a cobra. Yes, a little child will put its hand in a nest of deadly snakes without harm.

ושעשע יונק על־חר פתן ועל מאורת צפעוני גמול ידו הדה

Nothing will hurt or destroy in all my holy mountain, for as the waters fill the sea, so the earth will be filled with people who know the LORD.

לא־ירעו ולא־ישחיתו בכל־הר קדשי כי־מלאה הארץ דעה את־יהוה כמים לים מכסים

In that day, the heir to David's throne will be a banner of salvation to all the world. The nations will rally to him, and the land where he lives will be a glorious place

והיה ביום ההוא שרש ישי אשר עמד לנס עמים אליו גוים ידרשו והיתה מנחתו כבוד

Hosea 6, 6
For I desire mercy, not sacrifice, and acknowledgement of God rather than burnt offerings

כי חסד חפצתי ולא־זבח ודעת אלהים מעלות

Chapter 13

Jenny's Tale

Below is the story of Balaam and his Jenny (a female donkey). Balaam is summoned to Moab by Balak, who is afraid because the Israelites have camped there. After finally being given permission from God to go, Balaam sets out on his Jenny towards Moab. On the way, God sends an angel to stop him and block his path but only Balaam's Jenny can see him. Balaam's Jenny stops, and refuses to move, crushing Balaam's foot in the process. Three times Balaam beats his Jenny trying to get her to go, but she refuses. The angel of the Lord opens the Jenny's mouth and allows her to speak. She asks Balaam why he beats her so given that she has never done anything like this before. Balaam says it is because she has abused *him*. At this point, the angel of the Lord opens Balaam's eyes allowing himself to be seen. The angel confronts Balaam about beating and abusing his Jenny and tells him that if his Jenny had not stopped he would have killed Balaam but spared his Jenny.

It is at this point in the story that the common translation has led to misunderstandings of the text.

34
ויאמר בלעם אל־מלאך יהוה חטאתי כי לא ידעתי כי אתה נצב לקראתי בדרך ועתה אם־רע בעיניך אשובה לי:

This is generally translated as:

Balaam said to the angel of the LORD, "I have sinned, for I did not know that you were standing in the way against me. Now then, if it is displeasing to you, I will turn back." - The New American Standard Bible

Which is taught as - Balaam admits to having sinned, the sin being that he did know the angel of the Lord was in front of him. This understanding has many weaknesses the first being that, logically, the sin being referred to is the beating of his Jenny as that is the entire context and subject of this passage.

There are also translation issues in this passage that greatly affects the meaning. One being the word כי, which is translated as "for" or "because", however, it has many meanings including "although" or "but". Using these alternative meanings reinforces the fact that he is referring to the beating of his Jenny when he says he sinned but tries to mitigate his responsibility by saying he didn't know why his Jenny had stopped.

Another critical word is אשובה, which is generally translated as "to turn back" and understood to mean physically go back. The passage, therefore, is usually taught as "**I sinned by not knowing you were in the way and if continuing is evil to you I will turn around and go home**". The word אשובה, like all Hebrew words, is based off of a root word, in this case, שיבה means not just "come back" physically but also means **a spiritual return** and is translated as "**repentance**". For example this root is part of the word תשובה, which is used in several places in Deuteronomy, and means repentance and "returning" to God. Taking our previous discussion about the alternative meanings of כי and the root meaning of אשובה this passage is read as follows:

Balaam said to the angel of the LORD, "**I have sinned, but I did not know that you were standing in the way against me. Now then, if it is evil in your eyes, I will repent.**"

This translation make much more sense in the context of the conversation with the angel of the Lord and the several verses preceding it dedicated to Balaam's treatment of his Jenny.

The following verse, 35, has been artificially associated into the same paragraph as verses 31-34, however, as mentioned previously, there are no punctuation marks and verses don't even exist in the original Hebrew text. These groupings of words into sentences and sentences into verses and verses into paragraphs was all done by translators who did so for ease of study and teaching and convenience for the way they lived and thought. Verse 35 makes more sense as part of the next subject of Balaam's arrival in Moab.

Another challenge to the way verse 35 is generally understood is that, if (as is usually taught) Balaam says he will return because God does not want him to go to Moab, then the angel of the Lord would logically have negated his plans to turn around before directing him to Moab. The verse would naturally say, "**No, do not return,** Go with the men, but you shall speak only the word which I tell you." So Balaam went along with the leaders of Balak.

It is clear from the analysis of just this one sentence how much the translator's own prejudices result in tunnel vision and pervert The Bible's message affecting the way it is shared and understood by billions.

Numbers 22: 23-34

23
And Jenny saw the angel of the Lord standing in the way, with his sword drawn in his hand; and Jenny turned aside out of the way, and went into the field; and Balaam smote Jenny, to turn her into the way.

ותרא האתון את־מלאך יהוה נצב בדרך וחרבו שלופה בידו ותט האתון מן־הדרך ותלך בשדה ויך בלעם את־האתון להטתה הדרך

24
Then the angel of the Lord stood in a hollow way between the vineyards, a fence being on this side, and a fence on that side.

ויעמד מלאך יהוה במשעול הכרמים גדר מזה וגדר מזה

25
And Jenny saw the angel of the Lord, and she thrust herself unto the wall, and crushed Balaam's foot against the wall; and he smote her again.

ותרא האתון את־מלאך יהוה ותלחץ אל־הקיר ותלחץ את־רגל בלעם אל־הקיר ויסף להכתה

26
And the angel of the Lord went further, and stood in a narrow place, where was no way to turn either to the right hand or to the left.

ויוסף מלאך־יהוה עבור ויעמד במקום צר אשר אין־דרך לנטות ימין ושמאול

27

And Jenny saw the angel of the Lord, and she lay down under Balaam; and Balaam's anger was kindled, and he smote Jenny with his Stick.

ותרא האתון את־מלאך יהוה ותרבץ תחת בלעם ויחר־אף בלעם ויך את־האתון במקל

28

And the Lord opened the mouth of Jenny, and she said unto Balaam: 'What have I done unto thee, that thou hast smitten me these three times?'

ויפתח יהוה את־פי האתון ותאמר לבלעם מה־עשיתי לך כי הכיתני זה שלש רגלים

29

And Balaam said unto Jenny: 'Because thou hast abused (usually mistakenly translated as "mocked") me; I would there were a sword in my hand, for now I had killed thee.'

ויאמר בלעם לאתון כי התעללת בי לו יש־חרב בידי כי עתה הרגתיך

30

And Jenny said unto Balaam: 'Am not I thine Jenny, upon which thou hast ridden all thy life long unto this day? was I ever wont to do so unto thee?' And he said: 'Nay.'

ותאמר האתון אל־בלעם הלוא אנכי אתנך אשר־רכבת עלי מעודך עד־היום הזה ההסכן הסכנתי לעשות לך כה ויאמר לא

31

Then the Lord opened the eyes of Balaam, and he saw the angel of the Lord standing in the way, with his sword drawn in his hand; and he bowed his head, and fell on his face.

ויגל יהוה את־עיני בלעם וירא את־מלאך יהוה נצב בדרך וחרבו שלפה בידו ויקד וישתחו לאפיו

32

And the angel of the Lord said unto him: 'Wherefore hast thou smitten thine Jenny these three times? behold, I am come forth for an adversary, because thy way is contrary unto me;

ויאמר אליו מלאך יהוה על־מה הכית את־אתנך זה שלוש רגלים הנה אנכי יצאתי לשטן כי־ירט הדרך לנגדי

33

and Jenny saw me, and turned aside before me these three times; unless she had turned aside from me, surely now I had even slain thee, and saved her life.'

ותראני האתון ותט לפני זה שלש רגלים אולי נטתה מפני כי עתה גם־אתכה הרגתי ואותה החייתי

34

And Balaam said unto the angel of the Lord: 'I have sinned; for I didn't know that you were standing before me on the path and now, if it is evil in your eyes, I will return.

ויאמר בלעם אל־מלאך יהוה חטאתי כי לא ידעתי כי אתה נצב לקראתי בדרך ועתה אם־רע בעיניך אשובה לי:

Chapter 14

Offerings of the innocent

Sacrificing the innocent souls of animals, was always the pagan way and this practice was integrated into monotheism. The belief that taking the life of a soul, that happens to be of a different flesh, to achieve purity and to be closer to God is morally bankrupt. We can not connect to God through violence. When we do, not only are we trampling God's Commandments, but we are normalizing abhorrent behaviour.

There are many places in The Bible where we see clearly that God does not want and, in fact, never wanted "burnt offerings" (animal sacrifice).

Samuel 15, 22
But Samuel replied: "Does God want burnt offerings and sacrifices as obeying? To obey is better than sacrifice, and to listen is better than the fat of rams"

ויאמר שמואל החפץ ליהוה בעלות וזבחים כשמע בקול יהוה הנה שמע מזבח טוב להקשיב מחלב אילים

Isaiah 1, 11
What to me is the multitude of your sacrifices? says the LORD; I have had enough of burnt offerings of rams and the fat of well-fed beasts; I do not delight in the blood of bulls, or of lambs, or of goats.

למה־לי רב־זבחיכם יאמר יהוה שבעתי עלות אילים וחלב מריאים ודם פרים וכבשים ועתודים לא חפצתי

Here in Jeremiah 7, God is angry at the people of Jerusalem because they are sinning where he dwells and are doing so because they feel protected being in the Holy City. God, out of anger, tells Jeremiah they should not feel safe and that he will punish them if they don't change. He tells Jeremiah to go with other righteous people to pray for mercy but the people of Jerusalem continue to sin. God then, out of frustration, tells the people to go ahead and eat the meat from their offerings since that is what they do anyway and have obviously never fully shed their pagan ways. God says he only ever asked to be obeyed.

Jeremiah 7, 21-23
'This is what God Almighty, the God of Israel, says: add your burnt offerings to your other sacrifices and eat meat. When I brought your ancestors out of the land of Egypt, **I never spoke nor commanded them about burnt offering and sacrifice**, But this is the command I had told them: 'Obey my voice, and I will be your God, and you shall be my people. And walk in all the way that I command you, for it will be good for you

כה אמר יהוה צבאות אלהי ישראל עלותיכם ספו על־זבחיכם ואכלו בשר
כי לא־דברתי את־אבותיכם ולא צויתים ביום אותם מארץ מצרים על־דברי עולה וזבח
כי אם־את־הדבר הזה צויתי אותם לאמר שמעו בקולי והייתי לכם לאלהים ואתם תהיו־לי
לעם והלכתם בכל־הדרך אשר אצוה אתכם למען ייטב לכם

Chapter 15

Wood & Stone - Gold & Silver - Picture & Statue

Idolatry was a way of life in the history of nations. Monotheistic religions were not only fighting each other, but also those with polytheistic beliefs, like the worshiping of signs, multiple gods, and forces of nature through prayers, rituals and sacrifices. During the transition from a mostly pagan society, into a primarily monotheistic one, some pagan customs survived. God himself addresses this behaviour many times in The Bible and punishes frequently for it.

The deep need of ancient people to understand and make sense of the world around them, pushed them to create stories. The sun, the moon, rain, heat, drought, storms, volcanic eruptions and more were under the power of different gods. In order to keep their favor, strengthen them and get their blessings, serving these gods was necessary.

One of the ways they chose to connect to their gods was by building massive structures to worship them at and sculptures, made from wood, stone, gold, copper and steel to relate to them. Still today, images of gods of different religions and movements from around the world, which were created in the eyes and by the minds of mankind, adorn places of worship, homes, and even people themselves.

Just like other nations, the Hebrew tribes were still comforted by the idea of different gods and reluctant to completely abandon this way of life. This issue was one of the main things God had to deal with after he chose them to be his people. Disconnecting them from worshiping other gods was one issue, preventing them from eating living souls was another. In many places in the Torah and Tanakh, we witness God and prophets giving directions to the people about this very issue.

One way God tried to wean his people off meat was by making the eating of it complicated. For example, by commanding that it be eaten and sacrificed only at certain times, only where God designated (Ohel Mo'ed) and each one from his own flock and herd, never from others. Others, who did not own flocks and herds, were to sacrifice fruits and crops. Those who did not own land at all could donate money, and others donated whatever they had.

When people worship multiple gods, sacrifice living souls and perform sacrificial rituals (animals and mankind), God guides his people towards the way of life in the Garden of Eden. Meat and Flesh are always mentioned with a negative connotation when it relates to food. Fruit, seeds and Vegetation are always positive (fruit of the womb, fruit of harvest, etc), although they may be withdrawn or consumed by others if we disobey.

Deuteronomy 28

28:1-3

And it shall come to pass, if thou shalt hearken diligently unto the voice of the Lord thy God, to observe to do all His commandments which I command thee this day, that the Lord thy God will set thee on high above all the nations of the earth. And all these blessings shall come upon thee, and overtake thee, if thou shalt hearken unto the voice of the Lord thy God. Blessed shalt thou be in the city, and blessed shalt thou be in the field.

והיה אם שמוע תשמע בקול יהוה אלהיך לשמר לעשות את כל מצותיו אשר אנכי מצוך היום ונתנך יהוה אלהיך עליון על כל גויי הארץ
ובאו עליך כל הברכות האלה והשיגך כי תשמע בקול יהוה אלהיך
ברוך אתה בעיר וברוך אתה בשדה

28:4

Blessed shall be the **fruit** of thy body, and the **fruit** of thy land, and the **fruit** of thy cattle, the increase of thy kine, and the young of thy flock.

ברוך פרי בטנך ופרי אדמתך ופרי בהמתך שגר אלפיך ועשתרות צאנך

28:5

Blessed shall be thy basket and thy kneading-trough.

ברוך טנאך ומשארתך

28:8

The Lord will command the **blessing** with thee in thy barns, and in all that thou puttest thy hand unto; and He will bless thee in the **land** which the Lord thy God giveth thee.

יצו יהוה אתך את הברכה באסמיך ובכל משלח ידך וברכך בארץ אשר יהוה אלהיך נתן לך

28:11

And the Lord **will make thee over-abundant for good**, in the **fruit** of thy body, and in the **fruit** of thy cattle, and in the **fruit** of thy land, in the land which the Lord swore unto thy fathers to give thee.

והותרך יהוה לטובה בפרי בטנך ובפרי בהמתך ובפרי אדמתך על האדמה אשר נשבע יהוה לאבתיך לתת לך

28:14-15

and shalt not turn aside from any of the words which I command you this day, to the right hand, or to the left, to **go after other gods to serve them**. But it shall come to pass, **if thou wilt not hearken unto the voice of the Lord thy God**, to observe to do all His commandments and His statutes which I command thee this day; that all **these curses** shall come upon thee, and overtake thee.

ולא תסור מכל הדברים אשר אנכי מצוה אתכם היום ימין ושמאול ללכת אחרי אלהים אחרים לעבד
והיה אם לא תשמע בקול יהוה אלהיך לשמר לעשות את כל מצותיו וחקתיו אשר אנכי מצוך היום ובאו עליך כל הקללות האלה והשיגור

Below God outlines what will happen if he is not obeyed. Everything positive, seed, fruit, abundance etc will be ruined and not available.

28:38

Thou shalt carry much seed out into the field, and shalt gather little in; for the locust shall consume it.

זרע רב תוציא השדה ומעט תאסף כי יחסלנו הארבה

28:39

Thou shalt plant vineyards and dress them, but thou shalt neither drink of the wine, nor gather the grapes; for the worm shall eat them.

כרמים תטע ועבדתויין לא תשתה ולא תאגר כי תאכלנו התלעת

28:40

Thou shalt have olive-trees throughout all thy borders, but thou shalt not anoint thyself with the oil; for thine olives shall drop off.

זיתים יהיו לך בכל גבולך ושמן לא תסוך כי ישל זיתך

28:42

All thy trees and the fruit of thy land shall the locust possess.

כל עצך ופרי אדמתך יירש הצלצל

28:51

And he shall eat the fruit of thy cattle, and the fruit of thy ground, until thou be destroyed; that also shall not leave thee corn, wine, or oil, the increase of thy kine, or the young of thy flock, until he have caused thee to perish.

ואכל פרי בהמתך ופרי אדמתך עד השמדך אשר לא ישאיר לך דגן תירוש ויצהר שגר אלפיך ועשתרת צאנך עד האבידו אתך

28:53

And thou shalt eat **the flesh** of the fruit of thine own body, thy sons and of thy daughters whom the Lord thy God hath given thee; in the siege and in the straitness, wherewith thine enemies shall straiten thee.

ואכלת פרי בטנך בשר בניך ובנתיך אשר נתן לך יהוה אלהיך במצור ובמצוק אשר יציק לך איבך

28:55

so that he will not give to any of them of **the flesh** of his children whom he shall eat, because he hath nothing left him; in the siege and in the straitness, wherewith thine enemy shall straiten thee in all thy gates.

מתת לאחד מהם מבשר בניו אשר יאכל מבלי השאיר לו כל במצור ובמצוק אשר יציק לך איבך בכל שעריך

28:57

and against her afterbirth that cometh out from between her feet, and against her children whom she shall bear; for she shall eat them for want of all things secretly; in the siege and in the straitness, wherewith thine enemy shall straiten thee in thy gates.

ובשליתה היוצת מבין רגליה ובבניה אשר תלד כי תאכלם בחסר כל בסתר במצור ובמצוק אשר יציק לך איבך בשעריך

Kings 2, 6, 28-29

28 And the king said to her, "What troubles you?" And she said, "This woman said to me, '<u>Give your son and let us eat him today, and we will eat my son tomorrow</u>.'

ויאמר־לה המלך מה־לך ותאמר האשה הזאת אמרה אלי תני את־בנך ונאכלנו היום ואת־בני נאכל מחר

29 And we <u>cooked my son and ate him</u>. And I said to her the next day 'Give up your son and let us eat him.' But she hid her son.

ונבשל את־בני ונאכלהו ואמר אליה ביום האחר תני את־בנך ונאכלנו ותחבא את־בנה

In the past, eating human flesh did occur, sometimes for medicinal purposes and sometimes as part of rituals. There is even a well documented case of it by European soldiers, at the Siege of Maarat, during the Crusades. What is the difference between Flesh and Flesh?

The commandment Do Not Murder, does not distinguish between the kinds of flesh!

It does say clearly and accurately;
Do Not kill intentionally!
Do Not spill blood intentionally!
Do Not take life intentionally!

Chapter 16

Grass and Seed

As we saw in Chapter 14, God never asked for sacrifices or burnt offerings - only that we obey him. God, having dealt with mankind's weak and evil nature many times (Adam and Eve eating from the Tree of Knowledge, Cain killing Abel, the corrupted generation of Noah resulting in the flood, the Sin of the Golden calf, etc) decides that their evil inclination needs to be given boundaries in order for him to maintain some control. God directed his people to consume flesh as a way to contain their lust but restricted it to only "clean" flesh.

Only specific seed and grass feeding species, who have a calm and sweet nature, were allowed to be eaten and **Only** in the place God chose, which is The Holy Temple (known as **Ohel Mo'ed)**. Meaning, the only place God allows Meat to be eaten is in the holy place of God's temple, which is in ISRAEL.

Not at Home, Not at a Church, Not anywhere except where and when God designated; only then and there.

In Exodus, God gives the instructions for The Temple that he wants built in Jerusalem where he will dwell. God only dwells in his one and only sanctuary.

Exodus 25:8
And let them make me a sanctuary; that I may dwell among them.

There are many instances where God specifies where burnt offerings and other sacrifices are to be offered in relation to his Temple (The Ohel Mo'ed). In the desert, The Ohel Mo'ed referred to Moses' tent, which was God's *temporary* dwelling place until the final Temple could be built. It was to built in the Promised Land of Israel, in the holy city of Jerusalem and in the specific location today known as the "Temple Mount".

When giving instructions on how and where flesh could be eaten, we see God refer to the place where he chose and where he dwells. This is a clear reference to The Holy Temple in Jerusalem.

Deuteronomy 14:23
And thou shalt eat before the Lord thy God, in the place which He shall choose to,
cause His name to dwell there, the tithe of thy corn, of thy wine, and of thine oil, and the firstlings of thy herd and of thy flock; that thou may learn to fear the Lord thy God always.

ואכלת לפני יהוה אלהיך במקום אשר־יבחר לשכן שמו שם מעשר דגנך תירשך ויצהרך ובכרת בקרך וצאנך למען תלמד ליראה את־יהוה אלהיך כל־הימים

The Book of Leviticus and Deuteronomy give the exact list of Animals, Pure and Impure, Clean and Unclean. Between words and verses, the real instructions from God are laid down, but usually ignored. These are marked with bold letters.

Despite giving a list of "pure" animals, God makes it clear that he would prefer people not consume animals.

Follow the bold words and sentences.
Leviticus 11, 1-47
11:1
And God spoke unto Moses and to Aaron, saying unto them:

וידבר יהוה אל־משה ואל־אהרן לאמר אלהם

11:2
Speak unto the children of Israel, saying: **These are the living things which ye may eat among all the beasts that are on the earth.**

דברו אל־בני ישראל לאמר זאת החיה אשר תאכלו מכל־הבהמה אשר על־הארץ

11:3
Whatsoever part the hoof, and is wholly cloven-footed, and chew the cud, among the beasts, that may ye eat.

כל מפרסת פרסה ושסעת שסע פרסת מעלת גרה בבהמה אתה תאכלו

11:4
Nevertheless **these shall ye not eat** of them that only chew the cud, or of them that only part the hoof: the **camel**, because he chews the cud but part not the hoof, he is unclean unto you.

אך את־זה לא תאכלו ממעלי הגרה וממפריסי הפרסה את־הגמל כי־מעלה גרה הוא ופרסה איננו מפריס טמא הוא לכם

11:5

And the **rock-badger**, because he chews the cud but part not the hoof, he is unclean unto you.

ואת־השפן כי־מעלה גרה הוא ופרסה לא יפריס טמא הוא לכם

11:6

And the **hare**, because she chews the cud but part not the hoof, she is unclean unto you

ואת־הארנבת כי־מעלת גרה הוא ופרסה לא הפריסה טמאה הוא לכם

11:7

And the Pig, because he parts the hoof, and is cloven-footed, but chew not the cud, he is unclean unto you.

ואת־החזיר כי־מפריס פרסה הוא ושסע שסע פרסה והוא גרה לא־יגר טמא הוא לכם

11:8

Of their flesh ye shall not eat, and their carcasses ye shall not touch; they are unclean unto you.

מבשרם לא תאכלו ובנבלתם לא תגעו טמאים הם לכם

11:9

These may ye eat of all that are in the waters: whatsoever hath fins and scales in the waters, in the seas, and in the rivers, them may ye eat.

את־זה תאכלו מכל אשר במים כל אשר־לו סנפיר וקשקשת במים בימים ובנחלים אתם תאכלו

11:10

And **all that have not fins and scales in the seas, and in the rivers, of all that swarm in the waters, and of all the living creatures that are in the waters, they are a detestable thing unto you,**

וכל אשר אין־לו סנפיר וקשקשת בימים ובנחלים מכל שרץ המים ומכל נפש החיה אשר במים שקץ הם לכם

11:11

and they shall be a detestable thing unto you; <u>**ye shall not eat of their flesh**</u>, and their carcasses ye shall have in detestation.

ושקץ יהיו לכם מבשרם לא תאכלו ואת־נבלתם תשקצו

11:12

Whatsoever hath no fins nor scales in the waters, that is a detestable thing unto you.

כל אשר אין־לו סנפיר וקשקשת במים שקץ הוא לכם

11:13

And **these ye shall have in detestation among the fowls; they shall not be eaten,** they are a detestable thing: **the great vulture, and the bearded vulture, and the osprey;**

ואת־אלה תשקצו מן־העוף לא יאכלו שקץ הם את־הנשר ואת־הפרס ואת העזניה

11:14

and the **kite**, and the **falcon after its kinds**;

ואת־הדאה ואת־האיה למינה

11:15

every **raven after its kinds**;

את כל־ערב למינו

11:16

and the **ostrich, and the night-hawk, and the sea-mew, and the hawk after its kinds**;

ואת בת היענה ואת־התחמס ואת־השחף ואת־הנץ למינהו

11:17

and the **little owl, and the cormorant, and the great owl**;

ואת־הכוס ואת־השלך ואת־הינשוף

11:18

and the **horned owl, and the pelican, and the carrion-vulture**;

ואת־התנשמת ואת־הקאת ואת־הרחם

11:19

and the **stork, and the heron after its kinds, and the hoopoe, and the bat**.

ואת החסידה האנפה למינה ואת־הדוכיפת ואת־העטלף

11:20

All winged swarming things that go upon all fours are a detestable thing unto you.

כל שרץ העוף ההלך על־ארבע שקץ הוא לכם

11:21

Yet these may ye eat of all winged swarming things that go upon all fours, which have jointed legs above their feet, wherewith to leap upon the earth;

אך את־זה תאכלו מכל שרץ העוף ההלך על־ארבע אשר־כרעים ממעל לרגליו לנתר בהן על־הארץ

11:22

even these of them ye may eat: the locust after its kinds, and the bald locust after its kinds, and the cricket after its kinds, and the grasshopper after its kinds.

את־אלה מהם תאכלו את־הארבה למינו ואת־הסלעם למינהו ואת־החרגל למינהו ואת־החגב למינהו

11:23

But all winged swarming things, which have four feet, are a detestable thing unto you.

וכל שרץ העוף אשר־לו ארבע רגלים שקץ הוא לכם

11:24
And by these ye shall become unclean; whosoever toucheth the carcass of them shall be unclean until even.

ולאלה תטמאו כל־הנגע בנבלתם יטמא עד־הערב

11:25
And whosoever bear aught of the carcass of them shall wash his clothes, and be unclean until the even.

וכל־הנשא מנבלתם יכבס בגדיו וטמא עד־הערב

11:26
Every beast which part the hoof, but is not cloven footed, nor chew the cud, is unclean unto you; every one that to touch them shall be unclean.

לכל־הבהמה אשר הוא מפרסת פרסה ושסע | איננה שסעת וגרה איננה מעלה טמאים הם לכם כל־הנגע בהם יטמא

11:27
And whatsoever go upon its paws, among all beasts that go on all fours, they are unclean unto you; who so touch their carcass shall be unclean until the evening.

וכל | הולך על־כפיו בכל־החיה ההלכת על־ארבע טמאים הם לכם כל־הנגע בנבלתם יטמא עד־הערב

11:28
And he that bear the carcass of them shall wash his clothes, and be unclean until the even; they are unclean unto you.

והנשא את־נבלתם יכבס בגדיו וטמא עד־הערב טמאים המה לכם

11:29
And these are they which are unclean unto you among the swarming things that swarm upon the earth: the weasel, and the mouse, and the great lizard after its kinds,

וזה לכם הטמא בשרץ השרץ על־הארץ החלד והעכבר והצב למינהו

11:30
and the gecko, and the land-crocodile, and the lizard, and the sand-lizard, and the chameleon.

והאנקה והכח והלטאה והחמט והתנשמת

11:31
These are they which are unclean to you among all that swarm; whosoever doth touch them, when they are dead, shall be unclean until the even.

אלה הטמאים לכם בכל־השרץ כל־הנגע בהם במתם יטמא עד־הערב

11:32
And upon whatsoever any of them, when they are dead, doth fall, it shall be unclean; whether it be any vessel of wood, or raiment, or skin, or sack, whatsoever vessel it be, wherewith any work is done, it must be put into water, and it shall be unclean until the even; then shall it be clean.

וכל אשר־יפל־עליו מהם | במתם יטמא מכל־כלי־עץ או בגד או־עור או שק כל־כלי אשר־יעשה מלאכה בהם במים יובא וטמא עד־הערב וטהר

11:33
And every earthen vessel where into any of them fall, what so ever is in it shall be unclean, and it ye shall break.

וכל־כלי־חרש אשר־יפל מהם אל־תוכו כל אשר בתוכו יטמא ואתו תשברו

11:34
All food therein which may be eaten, that on which water come, shall be unclean; and all drink in every such vessel that may be drunk shall be unclean.

מכל־האכל אשר יאכל אשר יבוא עליו מים יטמא וכל־משקה אשר ישתה בכל־כלי יטמא

11:35
And every thing whereupon any part of their carcass fall shall be unclean; whether oven, or range for pots, it shall be broken in pieces; they are unclean, and shall be unclean unto you.

וכל אשר־יפל מנבלתם עליו יטמא תנור וכירים יתץ טמאים הם וטמאים יהיו לכם

11:36
Nevertheless a fountain or a cistern wherein is a gathering of water shall be clean; but he who touch their carcass shall be unclean.

אך מעין ובור מקוה־מים יהיה טהור ונגע בנבלתם יטמא

11:37
And if aught of their carcass fall upon any sowing seed which is to be sown, it is clean.

וכי יפל מנבלתם על־כל־זרע זרוע אשר יזרע טהור הוא

11:38
But if water be put upon the seed, and aught of their carcass fall thereon, it is unclean unto you.

וכי יתן־מים על־זרע ונפל מנבלתם עליו טמא הוא לכם

11:39
And if any beast, of which ye may eat, die, he that touches the carcass thereof shall be unclean until the evening.

וכי ימות מן־הבהמה אשר־היא לכם לאכלה הנגע בנבלתה יטמא עד־הערב

11:40
And he that eats of the carcass of it shall wash his clothes, and be unclean until the even; he also that bear the carcass of it shall wash his clothes, and be unclean until the evening.

והאכל מנבלתה יכבס בגדיו וטמא עד־הערב והנשא את־נבלתה יכבס בגדיו וטמא עד־הערב

11:41
And **every swarming thing that swarm upon the earth** is a detestable thing; **it shall not be eaten**.

וכל־השרץ השרץ על־הארץ שקץ הוא לא יאכל

11:42

All goes upon the belly, and **All goes upon four (feet)**, to **All who has many feet**, to **all swarming things that swarm upon the earth**, them **ye shall not eat**; for they are a detestable thing.

כל הולך על־גחון וכל הולך על־ארבע עד כל־מרבה רגלים לכל־השרץ השרץ על־הארץ לא תאכלום כי־שקץ הם

11:43

Ye shall not make your souls detestable with any swarming thing that swarm, neither shall ye make yourselves unclean with them, that ye should be defiled thereby.

אל־תשקצו את־נפשתיכם בכל־השרץ השרץ ולא תטמאו בהם ונטמתם בם

11:44

For I am the Lord your God; sanctify yourselves therefore, and be ye holy; for I am holy; neither shall ye defile your souls with any manner of swarming thing that creeps upon the earth.

כי אני יהוה אלהיכם והתקדשתם והייתם קדשים כי קדוש אני ולא תטמאו את־נפשתיכם בכל־השרץ הרמש על־הארץ

11:45

For I am the Lord that brought you up out of the land of Egypt, to be your God; ye shall therefore be holy, for I am holy.

כי | אני יהוה המעלה אתכם מארץ מצרים להית לכם לאלהים והייתם קדשים כי קדוש אני

11:46
This is the law of the beast, and of the fowl, and of every living soul that move in the waters, and of every soul that swarm upon the earth;

זאת תורת הבהמה והעוף וכל נפש החיה הרמשת במים ולכל־נפש השרצת על־הארץ

11:47
to make a difference between the unclean and the clean, and between the living thing that may be eaten and the living thing that may not be eaten.

להבדיל בין הטמא ובין הטהר ובין החיה הנאכלת ובין החיה אשר לא תאכל

Deuteronomy 14, 2-29

14:2
For thou art a holy people unto the Lord thy God, and the Lord hath chosen thee to be His own treasure out of all peoples that are upon the face of the earth.

כי עם קדוש אתה ליהוה אלהיך ובך בחר יהוה להיות לו לעם סגלה מכל העמים אשר על־פני האדמה

14:3
Thou shalt not eat any abominable thing.

לא תאכל כל־תועבה

14:4
These are the beasts which ye may eat: the ox, the sheep, and the goat,

זאת הבהמה אשר תאכלו שור שה כשבים ושה עזים

14:5

the hart, and the gazelle, and the roebuck, and the wild goat, and the pygarg (Dishon), and the antelope, and the mountain-sheep.

איל וצבי ויחמור ואקו ודישן ותאו וזמר

14:6

And every beast that part the hoof, and hath the hoof wholly cloven in two, and chew the cud, among the beasts, that ye may eat.

וכל־בהמה מפרסת פרסה ושסעת שסע שתי פרסות מעלת גרה בבהמה אתה תאכלו

14:7

Nevertheless these ye shall not eat of them that only chew the cud, or of them that only have the hoof cloven: the camel, and the hare, and the rock-badger, because they chew the cud but part not the hoof, they are unclean unto you;

אך את־זה לא תאכלו ממעלי הגרה וממפריסי הפרסה השסועה את־הגמל ואת־הארנבת ואת־השפן כי־מעלה גרה המה ופרסה לא הפריסו טמאים הם לכם

14:8

and the Pig, because he parts the hoof but chew not the cud, he is unclean unto you; of their flesh ye shall not eat, and their carcasses ye shall not touch.

ואת־החזיר כי־מפריס פרסה הוא ולא גרה טמא הוא לכם מבשרם לא תאכלו ובנבלתם לא תגעו

14:9

These ye may eat of all that are in the waters: whatsoever hath fins and scales may ye eat;

את־זה תאכלו מכל אשר במים כל אשר־לו סנפיר וקשקשת תאכלו

14:10

and whatsoever hath not fins and scales ye shall not eat; it is unclean unto you.

וכל אשר אין־לו סנפיר וקשקשת לא תאכלו טמא הוא לכם

14:11

Of all clean birds ye may eat.

כל־צפור טהרה תאכלו

14:12

But these are they of which ye shall not eat: the great vulture, and the bearded vulture, and the osprey;

וזה אשר לא־תאכלו מהם הנשר והפרס והעזניה

14:13

and **the glede,** and **the falcon,** and **the kite after its kinds;**

והראה ואת־האיה והדיה למינה

14:14

and **every raven after its kinds**;

ואת כל־ערב למינו

14:15

and **the ostrich, and the night-hawk, and the sea-mew, and the hawk after its kinds**;

ואת בת היענה ואת־התחמס ואת־השחף ואת־הנץ למינהו

14:16

the little owl, and the great owl, and the horned owl;

את־הכוס ואת־הינשוף והתנשמת

14:17

and **the pelican, and the carrion-vulture, and the cormorant**;

והקאת ואת־הרחמה ואת־השלך

14:18

and **the stork, and the heron after its kinds, and the hoopoe, and the bat.**

והחסידה והאנפה למינה והדוכיפת והעטלף

14:19

And **all winged swarming things are unclean unto you; they shall not be eaten.**

וכל שרץ העוף טמא הוא לכם לא יאכלו

14:20
Of all clean winged things ye may eat.

כל־עוף טהור תאכלו

14:21
Ye shall not eat of any carcass; thou may give it unto the stranger that is within thy gates, that he may eat it; or thou may sell it unto a foreigner; for thou art a holy people unto the Lord thy God. **Thou shalt not Cook a kid in its mother's milk.**

לא תאכלו כל־נבלה לגר אשר־בשעריך תתננה ואכלה או מכר לנכרי כי עם קדוש אתה ליהוה אלהיך לא־תבשל גדי בחלב אמו

14:22
Thou shalt surely tithe all the increase of thy seed, that which is brought forth in the field year by year.

עשר תעשר את כל־תבואת זרעך היצא השדה שנה שנה

14:23
And thou shalt eat before the Lord thy God, in the place which He shall choose to, cause His name to dwell there, the tithe of thy corn, of thy wine, and of thine oil, and the firstlings of your herd and of your flock; that thou may learn to fear the Lord thy God always.

ואכלת לפני יהוה אלהיך במקום אשר־יבחר לשכן שמו שם מעשר דגנך תירשך ויצהרך ובכרת בקרך וצאנך למען תלמד ליראה את־יהוה אלהיך כל־הימים

14:24
And **if the way be too long for thee, so that thou art not able to carry it, because the place is too far from thee, which the Lord thy God shall choose to set His name there, then the Lord thy God shall bless thee;**

וכי־ירבה ממך הדרך כי לא תוכל שאתו כי־ירחק ממך המקום אשר יבחר יהוה אלהיך לשום שמו שם כי יברכך יהוה אלהיך

14:25
and shalt thou turn it into money, and bind up the money in thy hand, and **shalt go unto the place which the Lord thy God shall choose.**

ונתתה בכסף וצרת הכסף בידך והלכת אל־המקום אשר יבחר יהוה אלהיך בו

14:26
And thou shalt give the money for whatsoever thy soul <u>lusted</u>, for oxen, or for sheep, or for wine, or for strong drink and for whatsoever thy soul asks for; and **thou shalt eat there** before the Lord thy God, and thou shalt rejoice, thou and thy household.

ונתתה הכסף בכל אשר־תאוה נפשך בבקר ובצאן וביין ובשכר ובכל אשר תשאלך נפשך ואכלת שם לפני יהוה אלהיך ושמחת אתה וביתך

14:27

And the Levite that is within thy gates, thou shalt not forsake him; for he hath no portion nor inheritance with thee.

והלוי אשר־בשעריך לא תעזבנו כי אין לו חלק ונחלה עמך

14:28

At the end of every three years, even in the same year, thou shalt bring forth all the crops of thine increase, and shall lay it up within thy gates.

מקצה שלש שנים תוציא את־כל־מעשר תבואתך בשנה ההוא והנחת בשעריך

14:29

And the Levite, because he hath no portion nor inheritance with thee, and the stranger, and the orphan and the widow, that are within thy gates, shall come, and shall eat and be satisfied; that the Lord thy God may bless thee in all the work of thy hand which thou do.

ובא הלוי כי אין־לו חלק ונחלה עמך והגר והיתום והאלמנה אשר בשעריך ואכלו ושבעו למען יברכך יהוה אלהיך בכל־מעשה ידך אשר תעשה

Chapter 17

Paganism in Monotheism

Words are hard to ignore, but actions are harder to change.
Everything is achievable and it depends only on the strength and willingness of the mind of a soul. As we have established and acknowledged, God has given us the recipe for purity.
A Vegetarian and Vegan way of life is much closer to, and fulfilling of, the divine laws.

People look at the words written in The Bible and accept the meaning as it was taught to them, instead of diving into the original text and discovering the real and true meaning within it. When translating texts, there are many ways to distort the meaning. This is compounded by the fact that religious leaders within communities must attract crowds in order to survive. This often leads to finding ways to interpret and teach The Bible that is most convenient for its members current lifestyle and which allows them to be most comfortable without having to make any significant changes.

This ranges from the integration of Santa Claus and other pagan symbols (Christmas Tree, etc) by some Christian Churches to the ritual slaughter of a lamb (Kourbania) of some Modern Orthodox Churches to the ceremony for transmission of sin by torturing and slaughtering chickens in Orthodox Jewish communities (Kapparot). Although these practices are neither required by the religion nor moral in nature, they are permitted, by those who have been given the moral authority to make decisions for the community, to appease the customs and superstitions of the community members.

Growing up, we learn that cows moo, eat grass, they have babies just like us, and they make milk. What many of us don't learn is that for the cow to give us her milk, it must be denied to her baby, who is taken away immediately after birth. For those who do explore this further, they learn that not only does the cow give us her milk, and lose her baby, but also eventually loses her life through violence.

We justify the Murder of an innocent soul, by saying god gave us permission, when in fact we do it out of Lust. Dominion to rule is a responsibility to protect and guard, not Permission to enslave other species. The truth is the cow is alive only for our 'want', not for our 'need'. In today's society we have no "need" to eat live or dead animals. Why do we "need" to Murder animals for their skin and fur? Where did this perceived "need" come from? In today's advanced society are we really "in need" of these things? Are religious people "in need" of murdering animals? For their flesh? For their skin? For their fur? For their Eggs? For their Bones? There is no need for these things to happen and there is definitely no need for Murdering the innocent! It is a perversion of The Bible's teachings to think one can connect to God through violence.

Murder is against God and It is against every existing moral code. So why are we still doing it?

Why are people Murdering innocent lives?

All sea and river creatures, Chicken/bird to its kind, dogs to its kind, cats to its kind, fox, coyote, wolves to its kind, mink, bear, moose, elk, caribou, beaver, raccoon, raccoon dogs, pigs, horses, elephants, rhinos, apes to their kind and many other innocent animals are enslaved and murdered for their:

Flesh - Meat
Skin
Fur
Eggs
Bones
Dairy

Justifying murder for the ridiculous claim that it is the way of the world, is absurd and wrong in every way. Paganism has never disappeared and can still be found in many aspects of Monotheism. God never asked for this kind of behavior and has attempted to prevent it with his rules and commandments. Every person who eats flesh commits the sin of Lust - Lust for flesh.

According to God, in Deuteronomy from the last chapter, even the flesh you could eat needed to come from your own flock or herd and then could be consumed Only in God's temple, which as we discussed, is in Jerusalem and no longer exists. And since God's temple does not exist anymore, there is no way nor do we have permission to eat meat!!!

Our commitment is not only to Stop the abuse of God's creations through not Murdering and consuming their flesh as food, their skin and bones as clothing, and their reproductive products (milk, eggs, etc) for our taste preferences, but to Stop the exploitation of animals entirely. While some are oblivious to the fact, many people know that Medicine, Cosmetics, Hygiene products and more, are tested in a brutal way on animals, both wild and domestic, before being sold in stores. Dripping an alcoholic mouthwash into the eyes of rabbits, attaching electrodes to the scalped head of a baby monkey, and vivisection are just a few of the horrific acts of abuse mankind is allowing itself to perform while ruling over other species.

Experiments on animals are done for the claim, they are very much like us. If so, could you imagine yourself going through these things just to satisfy someone else? Even setting aside the cruelty of subjecting 115 million animals a year to despicable experiments, the unreliability of these experiments and their applications for humans is now being admitted by scientists, researchers, and doctors alike. If you were to hear about Someone Poisoning animals of any kind to see what would happen, we would demand the maximum punishment for abusing the helpless creature. Yet we are silent when it is done on a massive scale and even supported by our taxes through government funding and legitimized by society as necessary. Why do we condone this through our silence? Should we give a hand to these acts of abuse by sitting at home, very aware that the products we use, were and are, everyday tested and experimented on animals?

Should we keep being silent when seeing clothing companies selling and presenting slaughtered animals' skin and bones in art galleries and fashion stores? Should we keep supporting tourism industries that make their money on the backs of animals? Riding animals that were "broken" (methodically breaking their spirit and taming them) and are now used for our amusement? How far will we go just to relieve our boredom? A boredom that exists because of our spiritual distance from the divine and his plan. Nothing speaks to this emptiness like gathering a group of people, young and old, to surround an animal that is caged and confined, not for his/her security, but for our enjoyment, while we make faces, loud noises, scream and shout, knock on the cage and throw things. Consider how excited the world gets when a wild animal is about to have a baby in a zoo. Now think about what it means for this animal who will be born, live, and die in Jail, never knowing anything beyond its small enclosure. This is would be like kidnapping a couple on their way to work, putting them in jail for no reason, forcing them to live there for the rest of their lives, while also forcing them to having children who will be born, live and die in jail to publicly amuse us. This will be the fate of this family for generations. These animals were not born nor created by God or our entertainment, but to live free in their own land as part of their own families.

How far would it go before we raise our voice and say… it is not ok!

Chapter 18

Mind over Power

How do we change?
How do we overpower our 'wants' and simplify our lives with our 'needs'?
How do we overcome the dilemma of changing our lifestyle?
How do we overcome the dilemma of changing our line of work concerning animals?
How do we become aware of what we are eating?
What are we going to teach our children and grandchildren?

Everything can be changed in a heartbeat! All we need to do is follow our decision all the way.
It is not hard once we have the courage of our convictions and the knowledge that we have no biological necessity to eat animal products (further evidence that God created us for the lifestyle we had in the Garden of Eden). Eating them is a habit not an addiction. Decide to open your eyes and realize that our lifestyle comes at the expense of God's innocent creations. Our ignorance about where our food comes from results in unimaginable suffering for the animals we've designated as "food".

Everyday, as we read these lines, innocent lives in the Millions are murdered for us to eat (billions of land animals and trillions of fish are consumed each year). Not only are these animals born with a death sentence but their short lives are miserable and full of pain. Many of these innocent creatures are cut and boiled alive (like lobsters who have complex nervous systems and feel pain) because it is the most convenient way to murder them. Some animals are tortured by being skinned alive due to the false notion that the quality of the fur is better and for practicality. This is not something that happens only in Asia, Western Companies who use fur trim on their coats use fur that came from wild coyotes caught in barbaric leg traps and are beaten and/or strangled before being skinned often while still alive and conscious.

We have come so far from God's plan for us, that when animals are fighting with each other due to intense confinement and stress, we resort to mutilation over giving them more space and treating them respectfully. Such horrific practices carried out by the Agricultural Industry include ripping tails and pulling teeth with force, castrating and abusing, cutting beaks with a 700 degree fire heat cutter, among many others. Another example of how disconnected we've become is how see male male chicks as simply a by-product of the egg industry because they will never lay eggs and are discarded by being ground up alive. Similarly, the veal industry was created to deal with the males calves that are useless in the dairy industry because they will never produce milk. They are confined to small crates where they can not turn around for a few weeks before being murdered. Another industry practice is called "Live Imports" where animals are shipped across the ocean crammed onto ships where many become injured or sick and are simply dropped over the side into the sea to drown, as was done to human slaves in past years.

In the most western "civilized"countries we are witnessing the use of horses for pleasure and when they "finish their job", they are sent to auction where Flesh traders buy them for pennies and end up being butchered for food. Once a little child's horse, later flesh on a restaurant's plate. In Asia, dogs and cats are stolen by the thousands and held in despicable conditions, where they are tortured and suffer excruciating pain, before being skinned alive and murdered for fur and meat markets (as of 2018 dog and cat fur can be imported, sold and worn legally in Canada).

They are butchered by the Millions every day in different countries. Using animals for our 'Wants' and not for our 'Needs' in many different forms is definitely not acceptable in any civilized society. Ever heard the saying; Humane Slaughtering? Since when is slaughter Humane? There isn't, and never will be, a humane way to murder someone who doesn't want to die. Flesh slaughter is a sin, but it is mainstream in our society. Religious and Secular people, as one, must change their way of living because our lust is causing mass extinction and destroying our world.

Mankind was born with an evil side, but was also given the understanding of good and the capability to choose. For secular people it should be a moral decision. For religious people it should be the decision to follow God's true way and be closer to divinity by doing so. Who gave us the right to use and abuse animals? We can not pray in church, donate money and Murder God's creations and think we are righteous. Doing so, contradicts our whole faith and belief.

Mind over Power should dictate our path in life. God's living creations were made to be ruled under mankind. The human brain is more developed making us more responsible for the quality of life on Earth, we should not be using our intellect for destruction. It is time to use every power of our mind and give up our evil habits of overpowering the innocent. The fruit of the Tree of Knowledge was in the Garden of Eden for a reason. Since we all possess the power of mind – we must put our mind over power.

Chapter 19

A Miscalculated Fairy tale

Once upon a time, there was a small herd of deer.
They had lived and died, by someone's commandeer.
One day, there was a loud noise of falling trees.
It was carried by the wind and shook their knees.
The next morning, the deer smelled a smell they did not know.
It was the smell of smoke and trouble as it show.
The deer were frightened and very much confused.
big scary flames of fire had changed their comfortable mood.
How did it happen, what was going on?
The deer were afraid and ran away from home.
As one full week had passed, the deer came back at last.
Recognized home, they did not, for it was black as night and hot.
The whisper of painful trees told them, go... go far and never come back.
You lost your home, go now, go straight and don't turn your neck.
The mysterious fire was not a nature's deed, but two legged creatures that claimed the land as 'need'.
Sadly, the deer had left and gone to search for another place they could call home.
From far they saw, creatures who looked like them, smelled like them and played like them.
They ran down the hill and met their kind, happier than before, resting their mind.
A day of one week, the herd had to meet, they missed a few friends and a strange smell came to greet.

What was it now? What is that smell? From far they had heard the fire bell. They ran yet again, to hide from the blaze, came back yet again and a weeping was raised.

What should we do? Where will we go?

Don't worry said a two legged creature and shot one with a bow.

Right away, the deer fled the place, where will they find their own land and space?

―――

The notion of controlling the population of deer by licensing people to murder them, is one example of mankind trying to overrule God's laws. When there is a group of deer in one place and they are forced to move, due to mankind's land taking, suddenly, there are "too many" deer in a different location. The group that was forced to leave, joined another group and the numbers of that herd got bigger. Hunting Supervision does not exist and is not possible, especially in far away zones and because hunters hunt constantly. This is exactly why there remains only 5% of the original numbers of Caribou. Many other "protected" animals became "protected" for the same reason.

Mankind is eliminating species without a second thought... "why else do we have a zoo"?

Chapter 20

The Creation Recreation

Since the beginning of mankind, there were always the two main ways of living:

the way God wants us to live
&
the way most people actually do live

In the eyes of God, the right way to live would be peacefully alongside all creatures of the planet, following a philosophy of "live and let live," where the life of an animal, beast and winged creatures is given the same value as the life of a human being.

The way we, as a society live, has been to brutally rule over and exterminate other species that are not considered smart or worthy enough or are simply in the way of what we have named "progress".

How can someone judge the intellect or value of another species, when each and every one was created differently not better or worse than the other?

People, whether, holy or unholy, religious or secular, moral or immoral, on the whole share a similar lifestyle. Many people think they hold strong beliefs about nature and the value of life but but very often their actions are in complete conflict with their beliefs, whether consciously or unconsciously. We've all seen a story on the news where several emergency personnel, news crews and good Samaritans, all come together to rescue wildlife from drowning in a frozen lake. It's a "feel good" story and everyone works together, sometimes even putting their own lives in danger to save the stranded animal. What we fail to see is that, very often, the same animal being rescued will be hunted by the very same people next hunting season.

Many see the needs and wishes of others, but ignore them and push their responsibility onto others. Many people find hunting repulsive and think it should it be banned because it is violent but have see no issue with paying for a cow to be bred through violence, raised under horrific conditions, slaughtered violently, then butchered, wrapped in plastic, and put on shelf in supermarket. Relieving themselves of the guilt by paying someone else to be the agent of the violent act

Convincing ourselves that "meat" comes from the supermarket and not from an animal, using terms like pork for Pigs, beef for Cattle, Veal for baby Calves, and so on allows us to make what is perverse seem normal and it is all done in the name of Lust and Greed.

Unless people change their perception of the norm and start treating each other and all creatures the same, nothing will change.
For the well-being of planet Earth, we need to raise awareness in the minds of all souls about how our current lifestyle is responsible for most of what is wrong in the world and convince people to change drastically and create a new "normal".

Higher authorities rewrite history and facts in ways that suit them and will draw huge crowds of blind followers, in the name of hope, safety, and salvation.

The Bible's true words were mistranslated and taken out of context, in the name of a false god, and caused the world enormous damage. Stories were twisted, to satisfy the Lust and Greed of those in charge and the people. These twists evolved into a way of life that took root all around the world. When questions were raised, they were quickly dismissed, to ensure there would be no interference on the path to re-creating creation.

Today, after thousands of years of adopting the way of sin, crucial and critical changes have to take place within all seats of power, communities, groups and individuals. Opening the eyes and consciousness of the world, will create a new world order, where the true word of God, flesh equality, is the law of the land and violators will be appropriately punished. Actions must take the place of words in order to create the reality all living souls should have been living since the creation of the intelligent world. No Animal, Beast, Creep or Winged creature will be sacrificed alive or dead to satisfy a human being's wish, tradition or will. The world's natural resources, if they are not consumed excessively, can take care of all the world's residents' needs. For example the water used to raise animals to be murdered and eaten by ONE person each day is enough water to grow plants to feed 14 people. The grain currently used to feed just "livestock" would be enough to feed the entire population of the world.

No Murder of other beings is acceptable in the name of humanity's wishes.
No experiments on nor abuse of other souls is acceptable.
Not by, through or in the name of God.
No Moral will ever justify it.
Religious and Secular people have to agree, acknowledge and put into action the changes that will cure the world from sin and evil.

In the story of Noah it is said;
God is good to all and has mercy on all his creations. Is Mankind above God??? Different interpretations and different routes were chosen and put in place, by people, to recreate God's recipe. If there is only one God and he has only one way, where did all the different denominations come from? If God's word is final, who gave people the permission to change it?

When choosing to follow God, we decide to obey his law and word. We can not change it based on our wishes and then claim it is HIS word. More denominations, more streams, more traditions, more false deeds and all in the name of the god we have created. The one who serves us and our needs, when we serve him. We use the god we created to justify Lust and Greed saying we were given his permission, which allows us to keep our twisted and evil ways. Instead of fixing a broken bridge, we just fill the cracks and put more weight on. We keep on lying and living the harmful lifestyle we have created. It is comfortable and serves our "needs".

The false "needs" we have created for our Lust and Greed. These "needs" can be discarded and wouldn't be missed. By choosing specific verses from different books of The Bible and combining them to tell the story we want to tell, we are creating a lie that we then live according to. We choose to follow blindly, instead of reading the whole story ourselves from A to Z and understanding the full meaning.

The Origin is in front of us, yet we keep on ignoring it!

Are we truly blind???

Ephesians 4:17-19

This I say therefore, and testify in the Lord, that ye henceforth walk
not as other Gentiles walk, in the vanity of their mind,

τουτο ουν λεγω και μαρτυρομαι εν κυριω μηκετι υμας περιπατειν
καθως και τα λοιπα εθνη περιπατει εν ματαιοτητι του νοος αυτων

They are darkened in their understanding, alienated from the life of
God because of the ignorance that is in them,
due to the hardness of their heart:

εσκοτισμενοι τη διανοια οντες απηλλοτριωμενοι της ζωης του θεου δια
την αγνοιαν την ουσαν εν αυτοις δια την πωρωσιν της καρδιας αυτων

Who being past feeling have given themselves over unto lasciviousness,
to work all uncleanness with greediness.

οιτινες απηλγηκοτες εαυτους παρεδωκαν τη ασελγεια εις εργασιαν
ακαθαρσιας πασης εν πλεονεξια

It is time to stand up and raise a voice
It is time to change our way of life and understand that humankind, animals, beasts, creeps and winged creatures, in water, land and sky, are all flesh and living.
Humankind can differentiate itself from the beast by actions.
Doing good deeds lifts humankind up in values and separates it from other flesh and blood.
Animals are neutral and do not choose things out of an interest to be above different flesh.
We have the power – let us use it with wisdom and the goodness of our hearts.

EXODUS 23, 2

You shall not follow the majority for doing evil, and you shall not respond as most to follow the mass to pervert.

לא־תהיה אחרי־רבים לרעת ולא־תענה על־רב לנטת אחרי רבים להטת:

Post Script

My name is Omri Meir Serper.

I was born in Israel into a Traditional Jewish Home and Hebrew is my first language. My loving and supportive parents encouraged and gave me the foundation for success in every aspect of life. I was always very spiritual and had a love for languages and this influenced how I read The Bible.

Since I was young, I wanted to work with animals, specifically horses and dogs. When I was old enough I started riding horses. Through observing horse trainers as well my own experience I became a successful horseman. I worked training horses for cattle working, trail rides as well as correcting problematic behaviour in poorly trained horses (in all cases the problem was with the horse owner and rider - Not the horse). Like most horse people and cowboys, I enjoyed consuming Flesh of all kinds; from Flesh of Fish, to Flesh of Chicken, to Flesh of Cow, Veal and Buffalo.

I never saw any problem with it, as the idea that eating Flesh was normal was drilled into me since I was a toddler. I lived this way for many years while considering myself an animal lover. Even when working as a cowboy, I loved sitting in the saddle watching the cows and admiring the life of the herd. Despite the admiration and respect I had for the cows, I never had a problem to have one of them on my plate at dinner.

For many years I didn't make the connection because it was a part of who I was, a part of the society and traditions I grew up in. No matter where I was while travelling around the world, I felt part of every place and every community I visited, since their lifestyle was similar to mine.

One day, when working as a cowboy for a well known cattle ranch, I witnessed the illegal hunting of an innocent 2 year old Baby bear who came out from the brush to pick and eat berries. This Baby bear was shot and roped, dragged and choked, heartlessly just to try out a new (and illegal), non registered pistol and for the "fun" of it. It was at this point that something in my mind was changed.

I was so triggered that I decided that I would change my entire lifestyle that day. I quit that job and launched a new career that did not involve exploiting animals. I changed what I wore and ate and I have never regretted making any of these changes. As I always had done, I looked to The Bible for wisdom and guidance. This time I approached The Bible differently; with eyes wide open and I was blown away by what was revealed to me when I read it for myself in the original unpunctuated Hebrew.

My life has only improved since deciding to live closer to the pure divinity level.

My life has truly changed from one side to the better one!

Made in the USA
Lexington, KY
22 November 2018